LOCOMOTION PAPER LP21

The Cleobury Mortimer & Ditton Priors Light Railway

by

M.R.C. Price

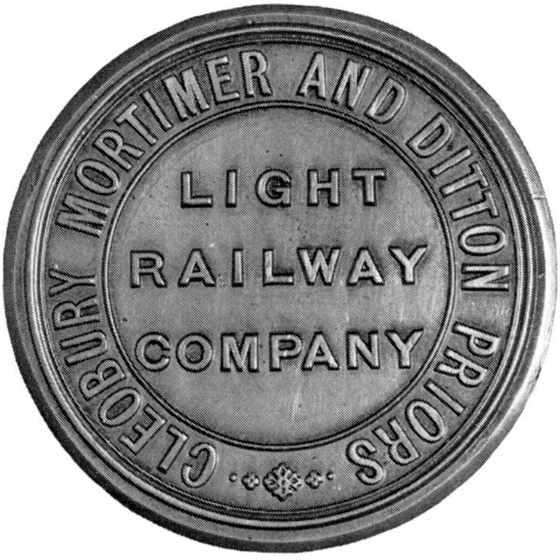

THE OAKWOOD PRESS

First edition 1963
Second edition 1978
New revised Third edition 1995
Reprinted with two new appendices 2019

British Library Cataloguing-in-Publication Data
A record for this book is available from the British Library
ISBN 978 0 85361 742 6

Printed by Blissetts, Roslin Road, Acton, W3 8DH

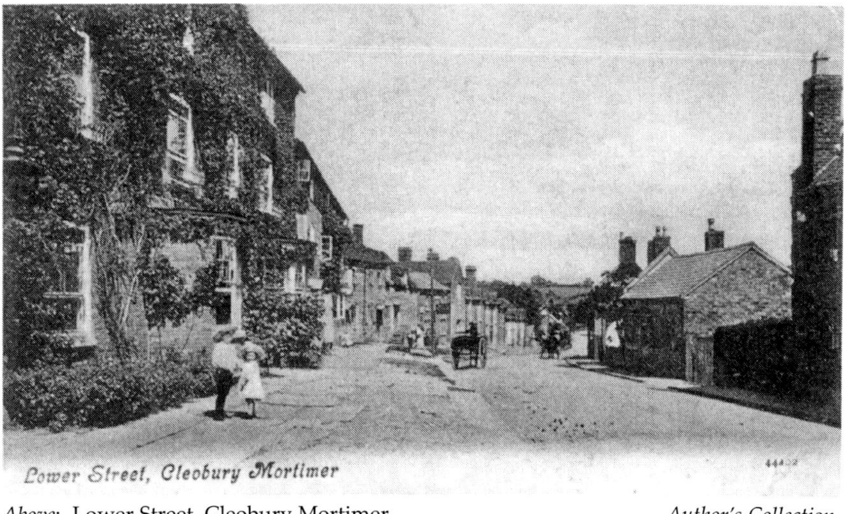

Above: Lower Street, Cleobury Mortimer. *Author's Collection*

Opposite: No. 29 with passenger stock (GWR replacements) at Cleobury Town. *Real Photographs*

Title page: Cleobury Mortimer & Ditton Priors Light Railway company seal. *GWR Museum/Thamesdown Borough Council*

Published by
The Oakwood Press, 54-58 Mill Square, Catrine, KA5 6RD
01290 551122 www.stenlake.co.uk

Contents

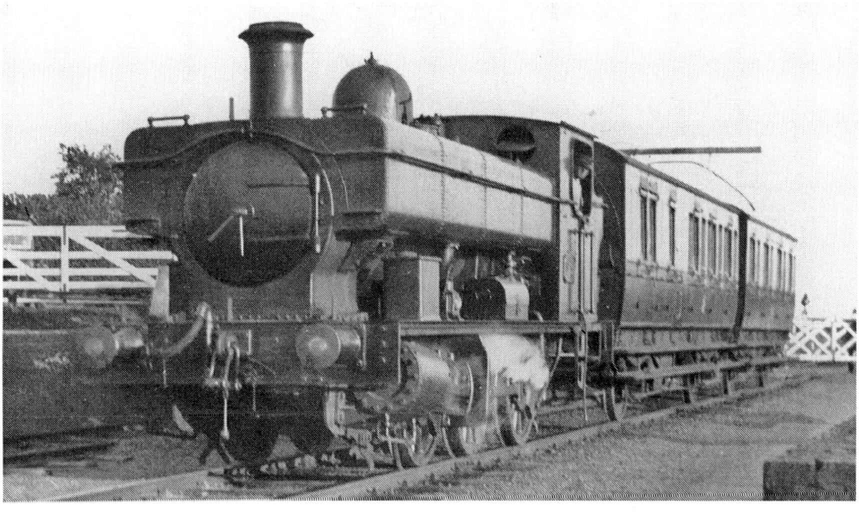

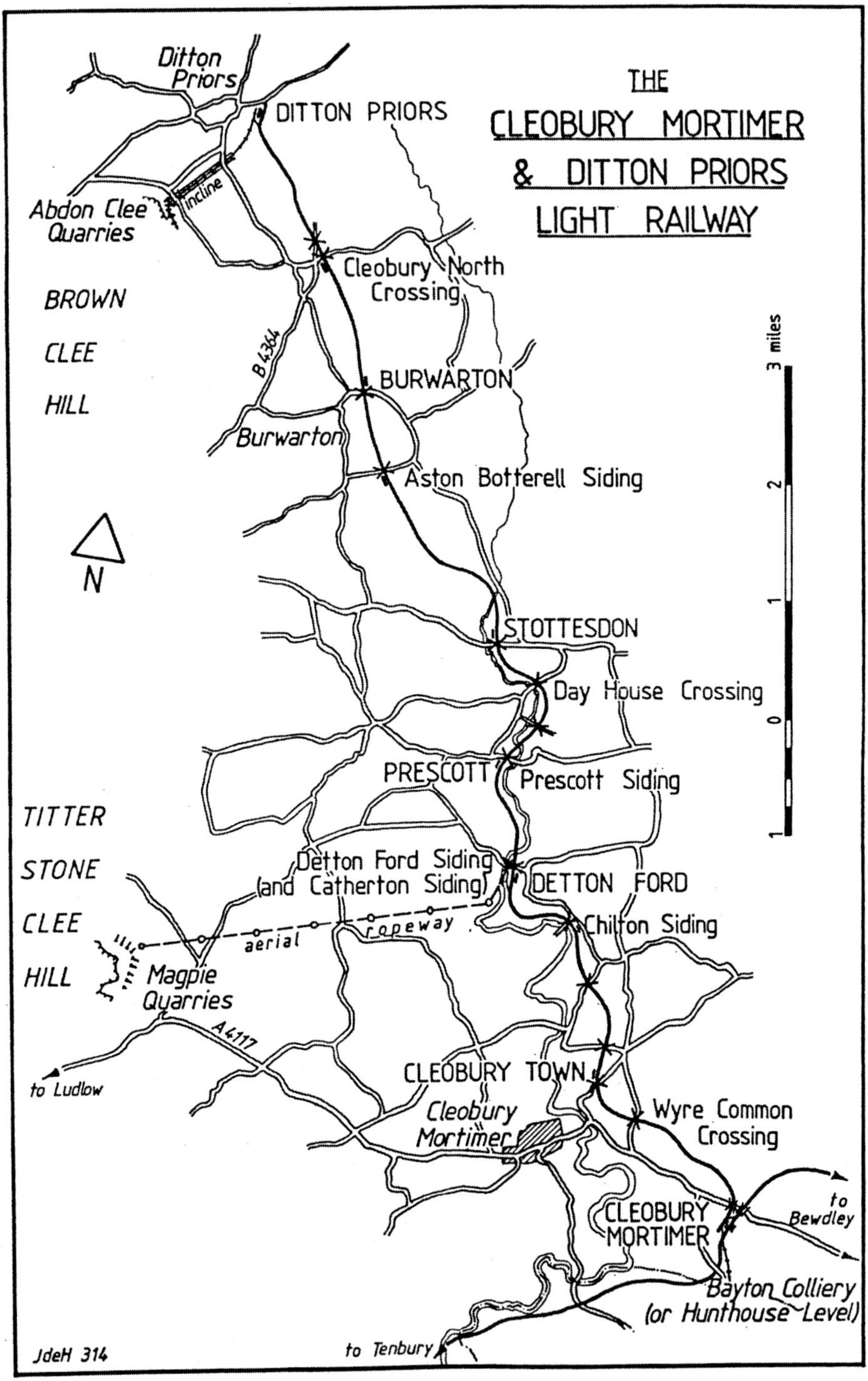
THE
CLEOBURY MORTIMER
& DITTON PRIORS
LIGHT RAILWAY
Ditton Priors
DITTON PRIORS
Abdon Clee Quarries
incline
Cleobury North Crossing
BROWN
CLEE
HILL
B 4364
BURWARTON
Burwarton
Aston Botterell Siding
N
3 miles
2
1
0
1
STOTTESDON
Day House Crossing
PRESCOTT
Prescott Siding
TITTER
STONE
CLEE
HILL
Detton Ford Siding
(and Catherton Siding)
DETTON FORD
Chilton Siding
aerial
ropeway
Magpie Quarries
A 4117
to Ludlow
CLEOBURY TOWN
Cleobury Mortimer
Wyre Common Crossing
CLEOBURY MORTIMER
to Bewdley
Bayton Colliery
(or Hunthouse Level)
to Tenbury
JdeH 314

Introduction

It is widely recognised that the railways of Britain are better documented than any other comparable home industry. The reasons for this are not hard to find, and certainly need no discussion here, but in this process it has been natural for the crack 'main line' concerns and minor railways of historical, technical or scenic fame to take the limelight. Just as some have been expatiated upon, others have been relatively ignored. This latter is surely true of the Cleobury Mortimer and Ditton Priors Light Railway. Yet its career, if not exceptional, has been one of variety, although the undertaking enjoyed one of the briefest periods of independent operation of any English line.

The railway's diversity, besides adding interest to the story, has also been of assistance in its writing, enabling it to fall fairly easily into sections. I only hope that the result may go at least part of the way towards remedying its former neglect. There have been many difficulties to overcome and discrepancies to sort out, and I must extend my most grateful thanks to all those whose help made this history possible. A full list of acknowledgments appears at the end.

Martin R. Connop Price
Newcastle, Staffs.
December 1962

Introduction to Third Edition

In the summer of 1962 I was privileged to spend a day on the Cleobury Mortimer & Ditton Priors Light Railway, courtesy of the then owners, the Ministry of Defence (Admiralty). The outing was so fascinating and enjoyable that, with all the temerity of youth, I set about compiling the first edition of this short history of the line. Later the limitations of that edition became increasingly apparent, and although the second edition of 1978 enabled a few improvements to be made, a more extensive revision of the text has had to wait until now. In the intervening years some excellent material on this little railway has appeared in print, putting more flesh on the bones of the story. The purpose here is not to duplicate that contribution, but simply to enhance and tidy up the work done in 1962/3, and meet a continuing interest in this small book. At a few points some significant alterations to the text have seemed desirable, but the basic structure is much the same. It is hoped that the new postscript and appendices will also add fresh points of interest to the story of this isolated light railway which changed hands four times in a career lasting less than 60 years.

As ever, I am most grateful to the many people who have in some way contributed information or other assistance to the preparation of this book, and most especially my family for all their help and support. A revised list of acknowledgments appears at the back.

Martin R. Connop Price
Shiplake, Oxon.
March 1993

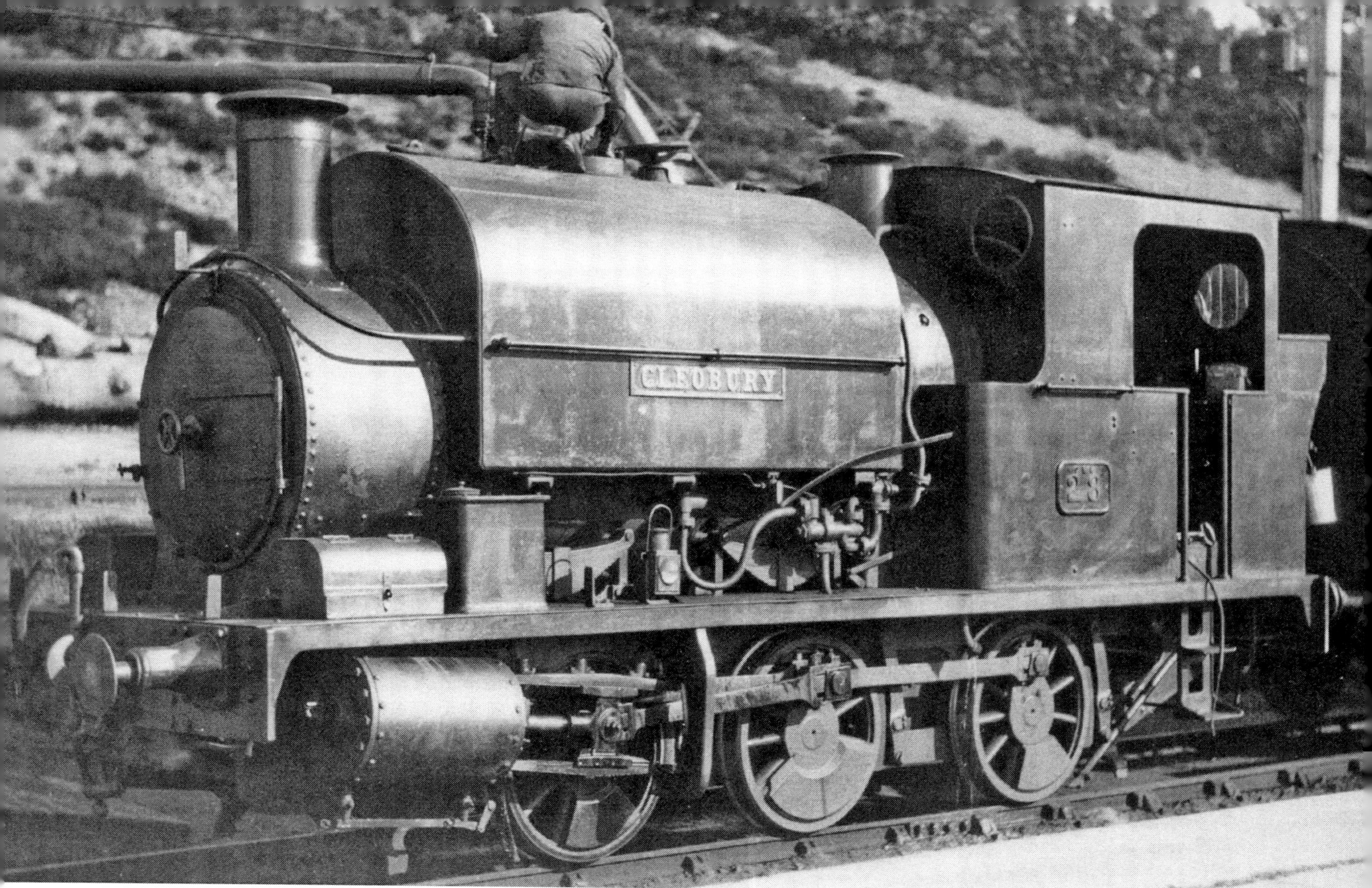

0-6-0 saddle tank *Cleobury*, fitted with GWR chimney, tool box, safety valve bonnet, and numberlate 28. *M.D. England*

Chapter One

Conception

The quiet Rea valley of southern Shropshire changed little during the 19th century. Essentially rural, its lack of proper communications caused it to remain virtually unknown to the rest of the world. Roads and railways grew up to surround the region at a distance, but no new project of any importance ever penetrated up the valley. It was not that local rail development was never advocated: such schemes as the Ludlow, Bridgnorth and Wolverhampton Railway would have cut right across the district. Unfortunately they were all too ill-founded to last.

There was some reason to consider railway construction in the neighbourhood. In addition to improving facilities for farmers, there was the prospect of mineral traffic. For many years there had been small scale coal and iron working in the vicinity of the Titterstone and Brown Clee Hills, on the west side of the Rea valley. In the later part of the nineteenth century this activity had given way to the quarrying of dhustone, a basalt which capped both Clee Hills, and which had become noted as an excellent stone for setts, and for road making generally. As early as 1864 a steeply graded mineral railway had been in use to move this stone down the western slopes of the Titterstone Clee, to Ludlow on the main line between Shrewsbury and Hereford. There remained a case for providing rail access on the eastern slopes of the hills to permit further exploitation of the dhustone.

As was the case in many other places, the Light Railways Act of 1896 turned what seemed to be an unlikely dream into a feasible proposition. By the turn of the century a number of local landowners and inhabitants were seriously considering the possibility of promoting a line up the Rea valley from the Great Western Railway at Cleobury Mortimer, on the Bewdley to Tenbury Wells branch line. Chief amongst them were Viscount Boyne and Admiral Robert Woodward, who between them owned much of the route of the proposed line to Ditton Priors. Indeed, the most important factor in the construction of the railway was to be the opening up of the extensive deposits of dhustone on Lord Boyne's estates. This traffic, it was estimated, would contribute £10,404 of the forecast gross annual receipts of £12,113. In addition it was hoped that the small collieries then operating on the neighbouring Kinlet and Chorley estates would be extended, and that new drifts or shafts might be sunk, utilising the coal leases that had already been granted. In keeping with the optimism which surrounded so many projects at this period, it was thought that these developments offered the possibility of no less than 200,000 tons of freight yearly. In the same way, agriculture was expected to benefit by the new outlet to markets, and it was supposed that the railway would encourage holiday and tourist traffic, sufficient eventually to enable the Rea valley to rival Malvern and Church Stretton.

Such prospects encouraged the promoters to arrange for the preliminary surveys. As a result, in 1900, Mr Everard R. Calthrop, who had been engaged for the task, produced the first plans and sections for the proposed standard gauge route from Cleobury Mortimer up to Ditton Priors, near the head of the Rea valley. As an engineer, Mr Calthrop is probably best remembered for his associations with the Leek & Manifold Light Railway in north-east Staffordshire, on which he must have worked simultaneously. His formal appointment as Engineer to the company was undoubtedly linked to the fact that the company Chairman in 1901 was Sir Alexander Wilson, who was a Director of at least three Indian railways, one of which was the Barsi Light Railway. In the event he was denied this opportunity of working on the larger gauge, but it does not prevent the most interesting speculation as to what might have been here.

Mr Calthrop's plans have a number of noteworthy points. The centre line of the railway is shown as being 12 miles, 1 furlong and 7 chains in length, with an average deviation limit of 100 yards on either side. The route was to rise a fraction under 300 feet from Cleobury Mortimer to Ditton Priors, with maximum gradients of 1 in 60 and curves no sharper than of 10 chains radius. The Rea was to be bridged near Detton Ford, Prescott and Stottesdon with spans of 30 ft, 40 ft, and 30 ft respectively, these being 20 ft, 15 ft and 18 ft high. (At this period Prescott was often referred to as 'Oreton'.) A further bridge was needed over the main road near the junction at Cleobury Mortimer with a span of 40 ft and a height of 18 ft. At other points alterations and diversions of roads and streams were proposed, and consideration was also made for the usual requirements of stocking up fences, the provision of drinking places for livestock and such like.

Meanwhile plans had gone ahead for the obtaining of an Order, under section 10 of the Light Railways Act, to construct the Cleobury Mortimer & Ditton Priors Light Railway. This was granted on 23rd March, 1901, and allowed three years to make the necessary compulsory land purchases, and five years to complete the line. £96,000 was authorised as capital, to be subscribed in £1 shares, with additional borrowing powers to the extent of one-third of the capital issue. In the following month the Chairman, Directors, solicitors and Engineer were officially appointed, and soon it was decided to seek estimates for the construction of the line.

The Great Western Railway, as owners of the existing line from Kidderminster and Bewdley through Cleobury Mortimer to Tenbury Wells, naturally followed the promotion of the CM&DPLR with some interest, but very little enthusiasm. Not sharing the promoters' high hopes, they did not rush to offer any assistance. In autumn, 1901, however, they did express a readiness to work five trains a day over the new line on weekdays only for 2*s.* per train mile. Alternatively they said they would be willing to take 60 per cent of the gross receipts, plus an indemnity in respect of their expenses. This was not well received by the Directors, especially as Lord Boyne was unwilling to increase his financial commitment to the scheme simply to satisfy the demands of the GWR.

In March 1902, a tender of £100,000 to build the railway was received from J.T. Firbank & Co., and the chances of some progress seemed to be improved. Unfortunately the company continued to face financial difficulties, and could

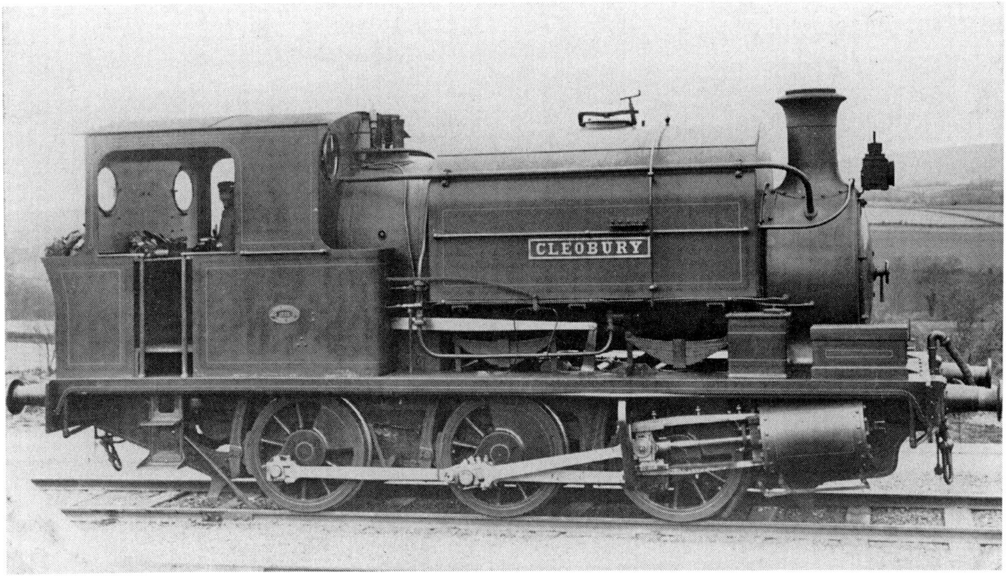

Cleobury in original condition. *Locomotive Publishing Co./Oakwood Collection*

Cleobury and goods brake No. 2 *Locomotive Publishing Co./Oakwood Collection*

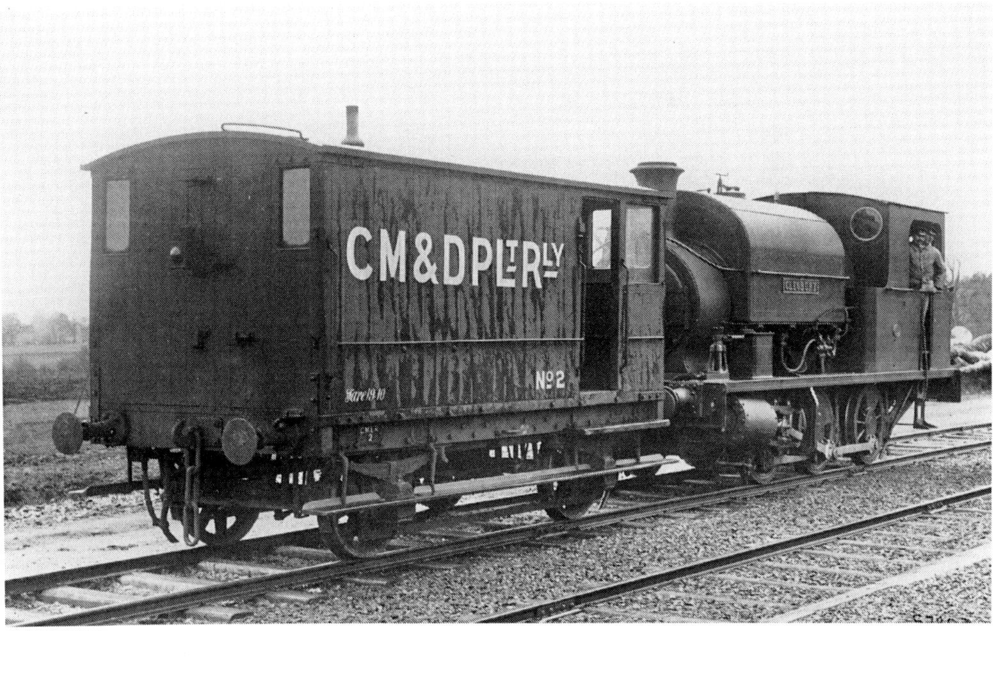

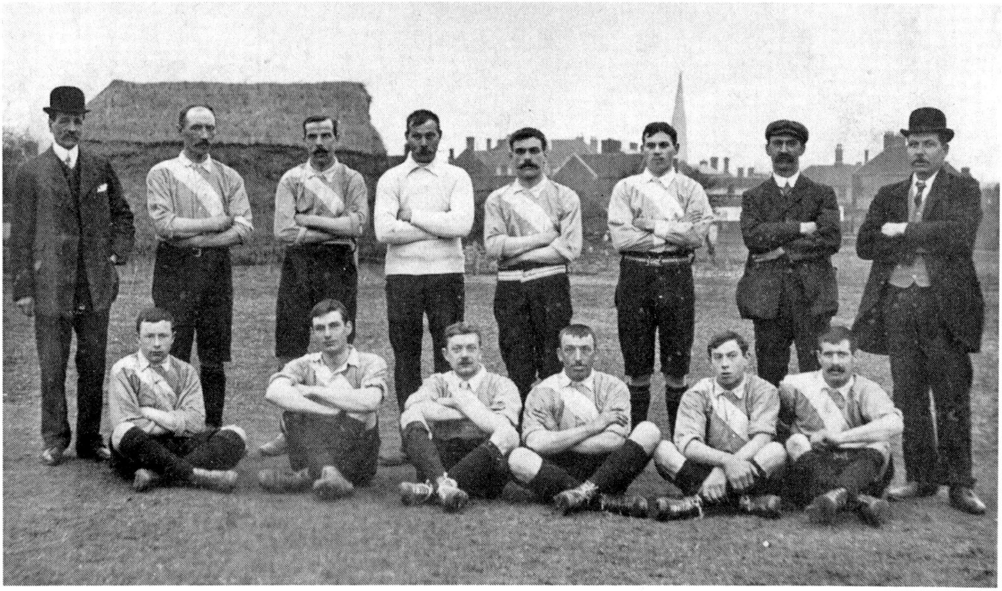

The CM&DPLR football team, the CM&DPR manager Mr E. Morris is on the far left.
N. How Collection

Cleobury with a mixed train at Cleobury Mortimer Junction, 1st May, 1920.
K.A.C.R. Nunn/LCGB

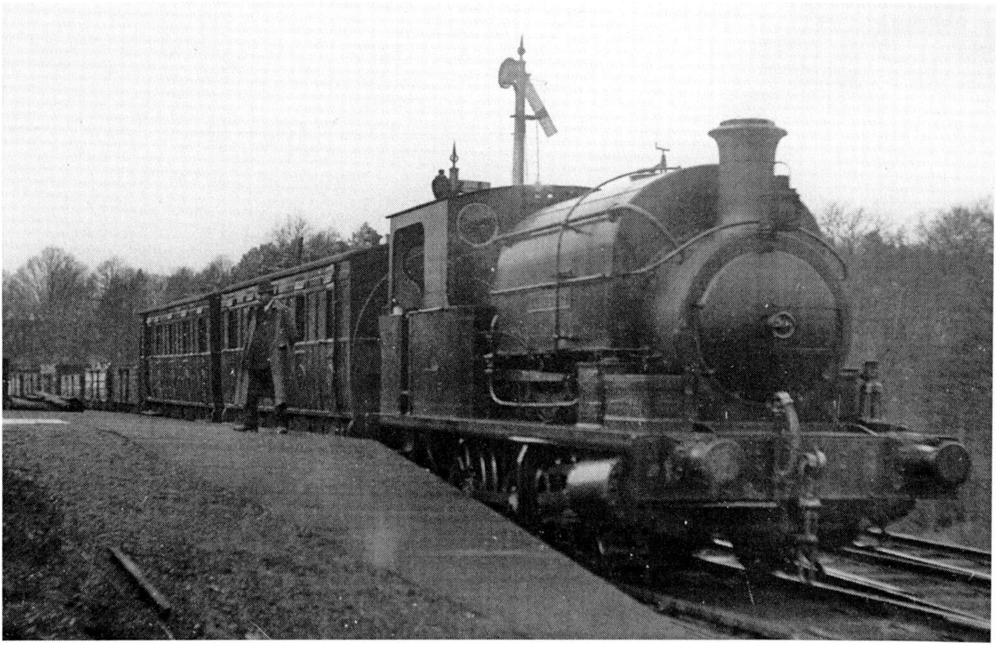

not reach an agreement with these contractors. Notwithstanding receipt of two more tenders in 1903, no agreement on construction was possible. Tiring of the delays, Sir Alexander Wilson and one other Director resigned in 1904; their replacements on the Board resigned in turn in 1905. As Lord Boyne remained reluctant to subscribe more money to the venture, no further progress was made until 1906.

In January 1906, the company solicitor produced a scheme for the provision of capital and the construction of the railway by a Mr George Law, of Kidderminster. This contractor had submitted a tender of £86,500 for the work, to be completed in twelve months. Payment was to be by way of £48,000 in cash and £38,500 in shares, and the total included £7,000 to cover the cost of two locomotives, carriages, wagons, signals, telegraphs, crane, weighbridges and water supply. Mr Law also asked that he be free to select his own Engineer to replace Mr Calthrop, and, with some regret, this was agreed by the CM&DP Board, even though the construction contract had not been signed. The new Engineer was Mr William T. Foxlee. The Board, in its turn, specifically asked Mr Law to ensure that the Abdon Clee dhustone quarry should be active prior to the opening of the railway.

Although these arrangements appeared promising early in 1906, there were some pitfalls ahead. The Board of Trade was persuaded to grant an extension of time for the building of the railway, but increasingly indicated their concern over the delays and protracted discussions. In May 1906, the CM&DP Directors were unhappy to learn that Mr Law could not promise to bring the Abdon Clee quarry into use before completion of the railway. Frustrated by Mr Law's hesitations over the contract, the company broke off negotiations in June. As if this were not enough, matters were complicated even more by the first Secretary of the company, a Mr Polglasse, going bankrupt.

If this was the bad news, the good news arrived in the form of the contractors Messrs Bott & Stennett. No sooner had Mr Law departed from the scene than they appeared with a similar contract, also for £86,500. The provisions included the interesting proposal that while the line was under construction Mr William Clarke Stennett of the contractors should be appointed a Director of the railway at £100 per annum. Initially the company Chairman, Mr Spencer Gore Brown, viewed this with disfavour, but the relationship was to prove to be beneficial. Even more surprising was the Board's acceptance of Mr Stennett's statement in September 1906, that he would not be able to open the quarry before completing the line. At this point the Directors in general, and Lord Boyne in particular, must have felt that there had been delays enough, and in the same month Lord Boyne agreed to subscribe £35,000 in £1 shares, thereby enabling the contract to be let. At long last the construction of the Cleobury Mortimer & Ditton Priors Light Railway could begin.

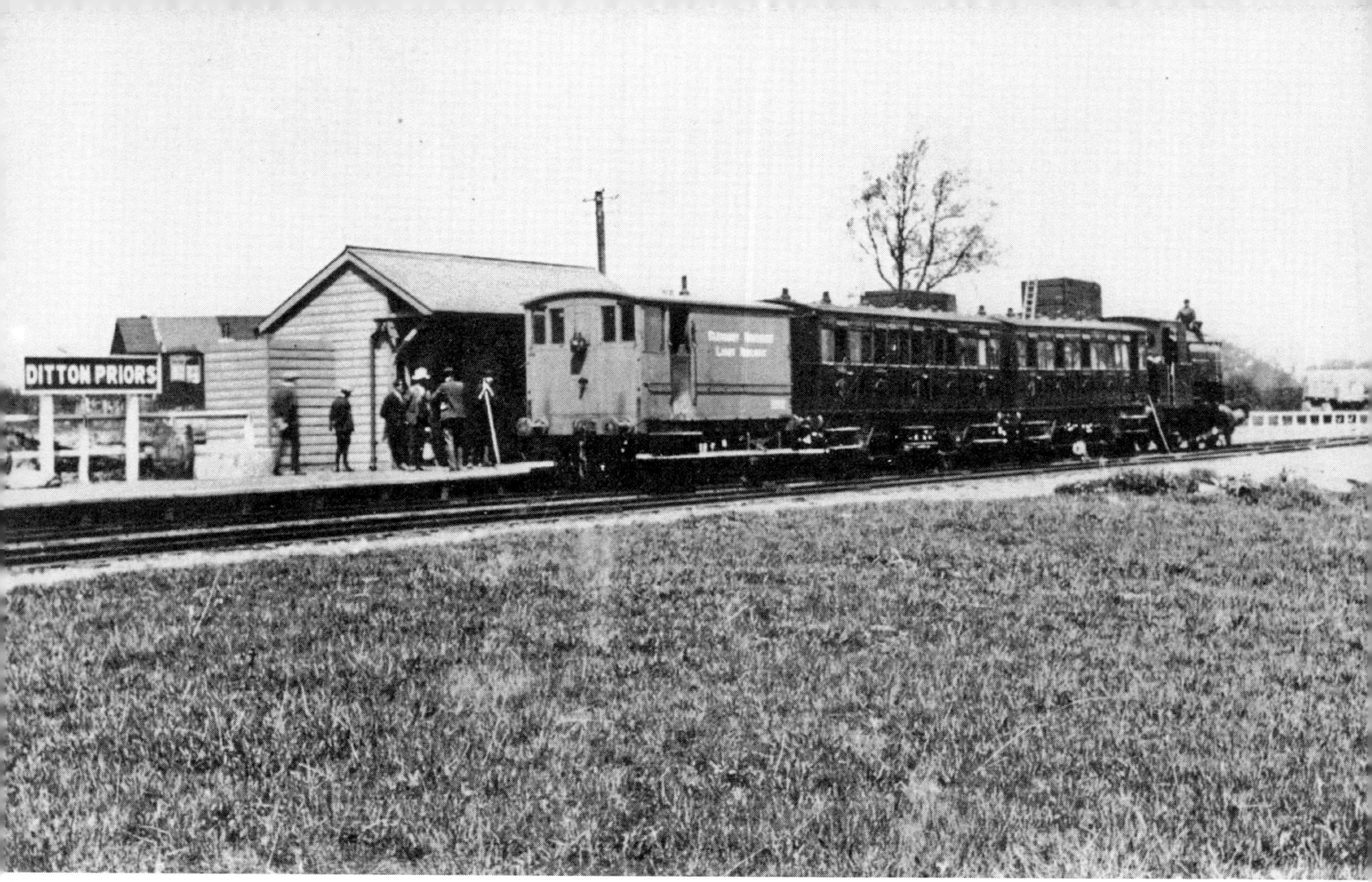

Ditton Priors station in the early years of the railway. Note the original timber-built tank supplying water to the engine. *R.C. Riley Collection*

Chapter Two

Construction

Under the terms of the agreement between Messrs Bott & Stennett and the CM&DPLR in September 1906, the contractors were required to create a distinct company to quarry the dhustone, as well as provide a rail connection between the deposit and Ditton Priors. The lease for the development of the stone was granted by Lord Boyne the day after the contract for the construction of the CM&DP was signed. These links between the quarry concern, which came to be called the Abdon Clee Stone Quarry Co. Ltd, and the railway were further strengthened by the appointment of several of those responsible for the undertakings (including the contractor) as Directors of both, and by the fact that two-thirds of the debentures and shares of the quarry were eventually held by the principal shareholders and Directors of the CM&DPLR.

Meanwhile the new Engineer, Mr Foxlee, had decided some of Mr Calthrop's plans and sections required modification. In particular, the junction with the GWR at Cleobury Mortimer was moved a little to the north, making the exchange of passengers for the light railway more convenient, and slightly shortening the overall length of the line. No radical change was made elsewhere on the route of the railway, although some small realignments of its centre line took place. In addition Mr Foxlee altered the sections so that the track followed the contours even more closely than it had done previously, with more frequent changes of gradient. The limit for the curves and grades did, however, remain at 10 chains radius and 1 in 60 respectively. In January 1907, Mr Foxlee gave the Board of Trade details of the proposed realignment at and near Cleobury Mortimer Junction, and advised that Shropshire County Council had agreed on the understanding that two level crossings (at Cleobury Town and Cleobury North) be improved. The Board of Trade duly consented to the new arrangements.

The actual clearance work began as soon as the contractors took possession of the required land near Cleobury Mortimer at the end of January 1907, and within about a fortnight all the land necessary for the first two miles had been obtained. All in all some 67 acres were needed for the railway, 35½ of which were already in the possession of well-wishers of the CM&DPLR. The remainder was taken over after a number of those interesting claims by landowners that often accompany constructional works. Most were simply for loss of crops and disturbance, but one tried unsuccessfully to compel the company to build a halt on a portion of the property to be purchased, whilst another obliged the CM&DP to obtain a right of way for his cattle over a road belonging to a neighbouring farmer. A third and most surprising of all, demanded £50 for disturbance and loss of rabbits!

None of these claims presented an insuperable problem, and building of the line proceeded steadily. Considering the modest length of the line, Messrs Bott & Stennett brought in a considerable amount of plant for the job. A steam navvy was soon at work excavating cuttings between Cleobury

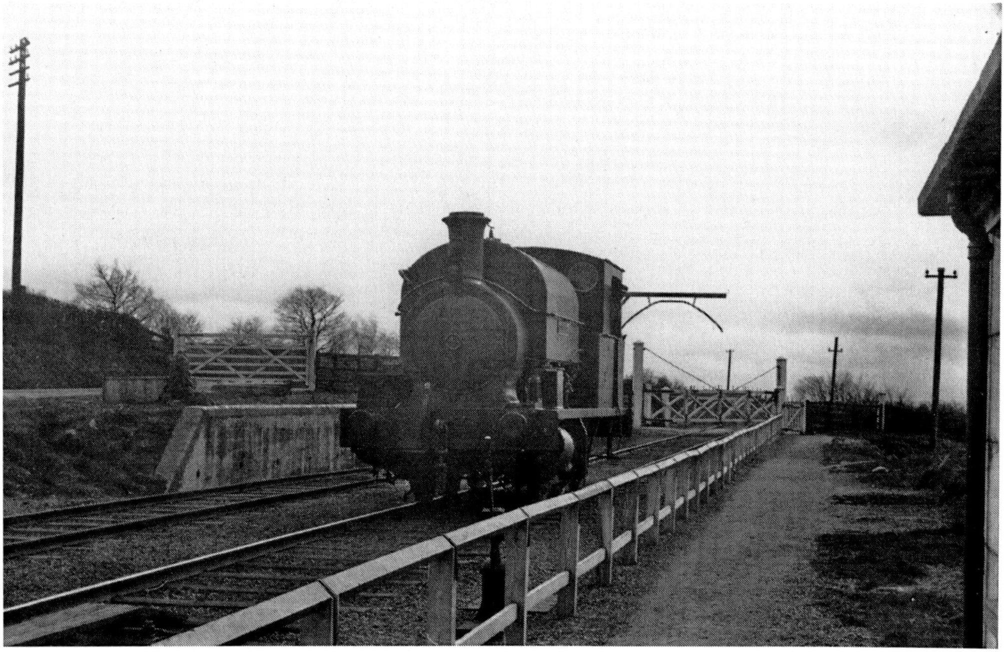

Cleobury pauses at Cleobury Town. *Locomotive Publishing Co./Oakwood Collection*

Cleobury and mixed train arriving at Cleobury Town on 1st May, 1920. *K.A.C.R. Nunn/LCGB*

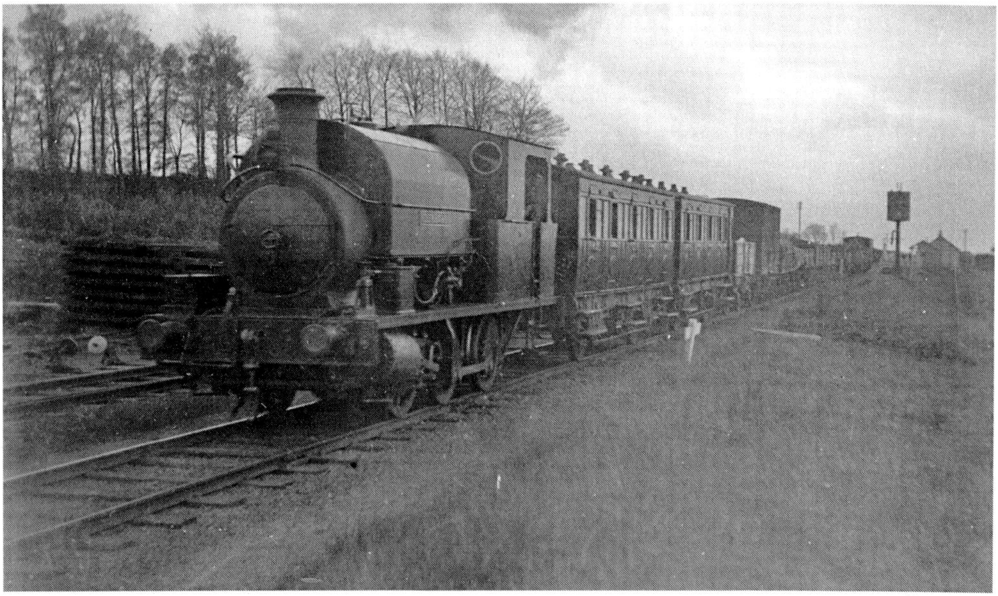

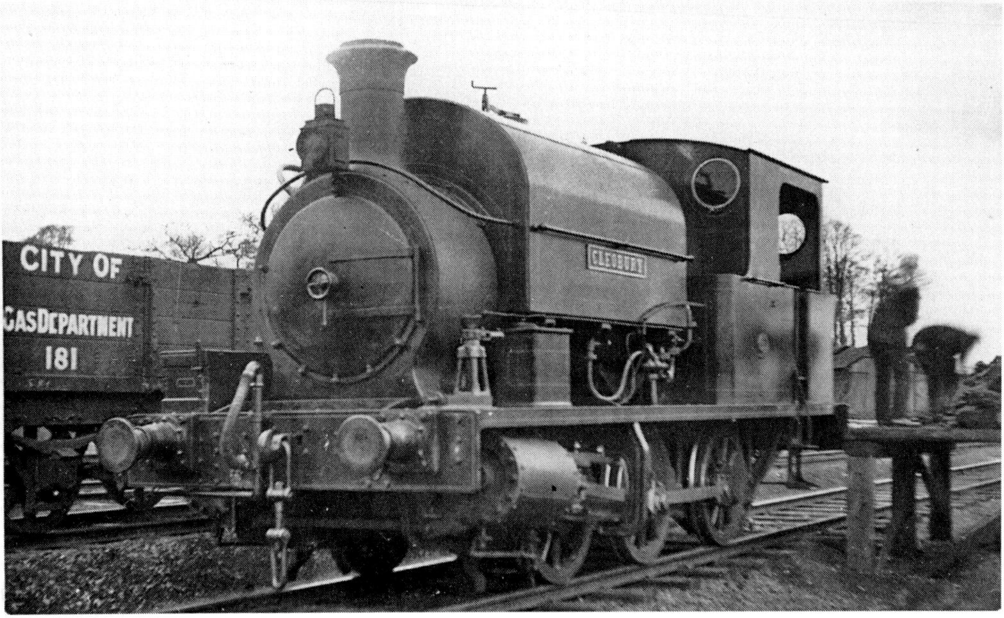

Coaling *Cleobury* at Cleobury Town, May 1920. *K.A.C.R. Nunn/LCGB*

Cleobury and mixed train arrive at Cleobury Town in May 1920. *K.A.C.R. Nunn/LCGB*

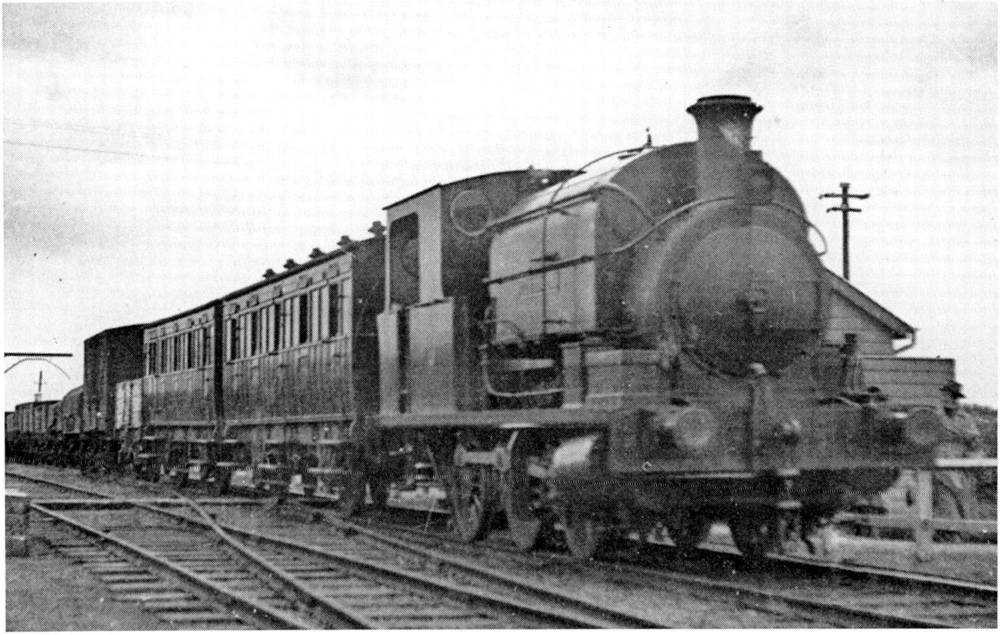

Mortimer Junction and Cleobury Town, and several locomotives were employed to move spoil, stone and materials along the works. By mid-summer some work had been put in hand on most parts of the route, but much correspondence was required to obtain Board of Trade consent to further extensions of time for the completion of the line. The date was adjusted to 23rd May, 1908, and then later to 23rd November, 1908.

In July 1907, the Light Railway Commissioners held a public inquiry at Bewdley into an application for the construction of a light railway running in a north-easterly direction for 5½ miles from Stottesdon to Kinlet and Billingsley. The main purpose of this scheme was to provide an outlet for coal from the Billingsley colliery, operated in conjunction with the CM&DPLR. Although the idea was welcomed by the latter, and won the support of the Commissioners, it came to nothing. Following a change in the ownership of the Billingsley colliery, it was decided to link it directly to the GWR's Severn Valley line, and work began on this connection in 1908.

As work on building the CM&DP forged ahead, progress was marred at the close of 1907 by the death of Lord Boyne. The railway was, in a sense, almost his railway, and it was indeed unfortunate that he never saw it opened. However, he must have known that the route was nearing completion, and that the last lengths of track were about to be laid.

In May 1908, there was additional sadness with news of an accident on the Abdon Clee quarry incline, then nearing completion, whereby a driver of one of the contractors' locomotives was killed. Two locomotives had been struggling to propel a wagon of ashes up the incline but stalled at a point where the incline was reported to be 1 in 13. Both engines slid backwards, swaying, and derailed. Although they remained upright it seems that the driver of the second locomotive, Driver Revell, was thrown onto the track and killed by the first locomotive as it slipped backwards.

These setbacks apart, the work continued, and in July 1908, the railway was ready for traffic. From the first of that month preliminary use was made of part of the route, and on the 19th a daily freight train over the whole length of the line was commenced. Motive power was initially provided by the contractors' 0-6-0 saddle tank, *Fleetwood* on hire, the two locomotives ordered for regular operation on the CM&DPLR not then having been delivered. In the meantime work proceeded in putting the rest of the equipment into good order in preparation for the Board of Trade inspection, which was fixed for 13th November, 1908.

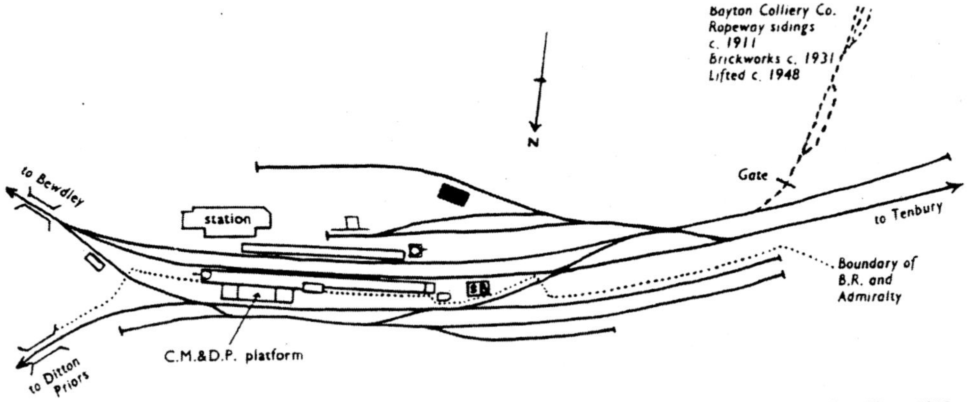

CLEOBURY MORTIMER c. 1960

CLEOBURY TOWN

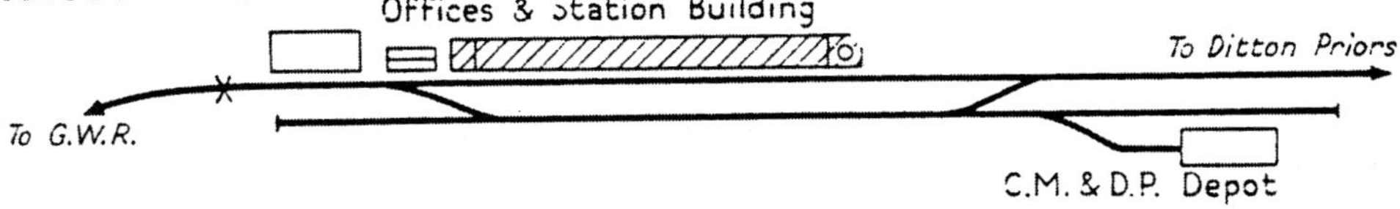

STOTTESDON

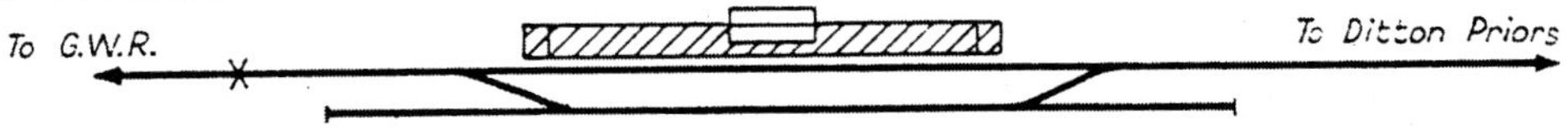

BURWARTON

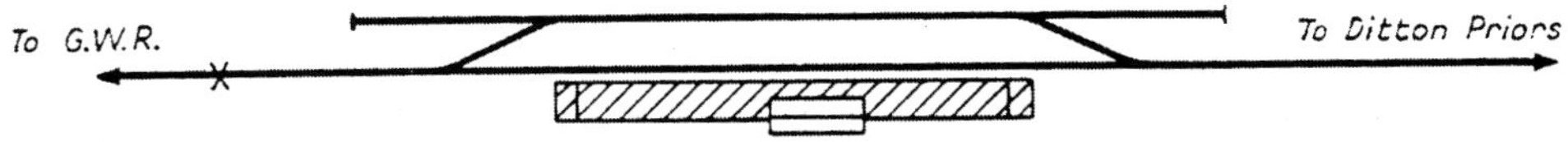

DITTON PRIORS

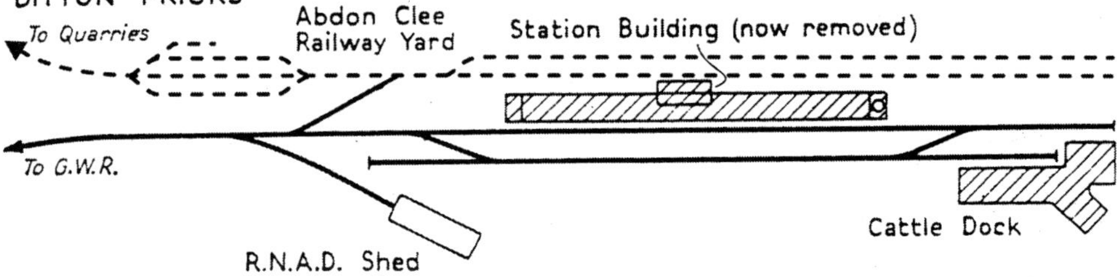

JRB

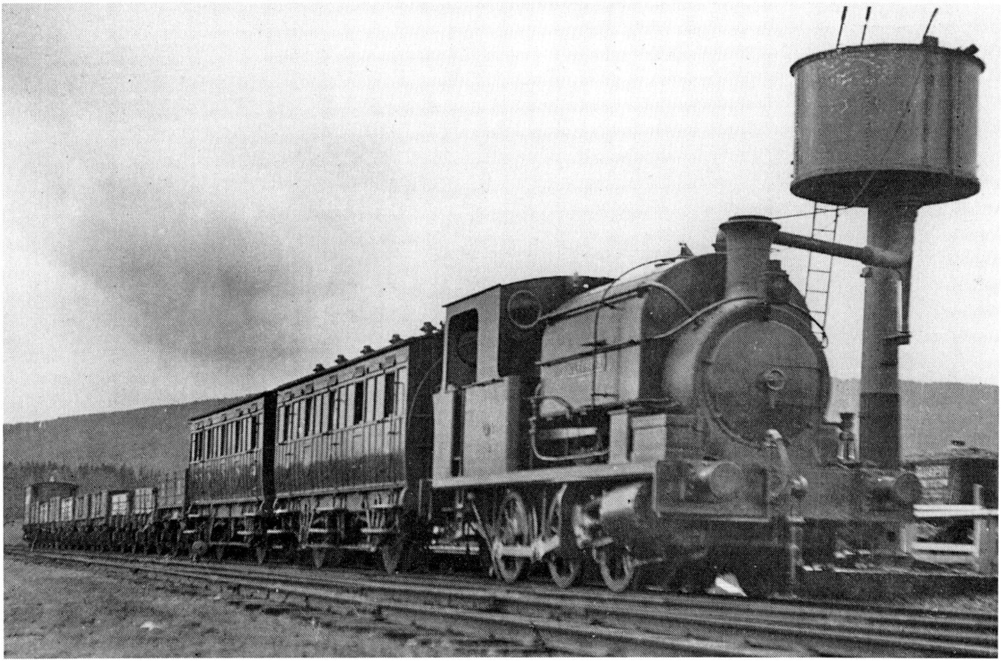

Cleobury takes water on arrival at Ditton Priors, 1st May, 1920. *K.A.C.R. Nunn/LCGB*

Cleobury prepares to leave Ditton Priors with a mixed train, May 1920. *K.A.C.R. Nunn/LCGB*

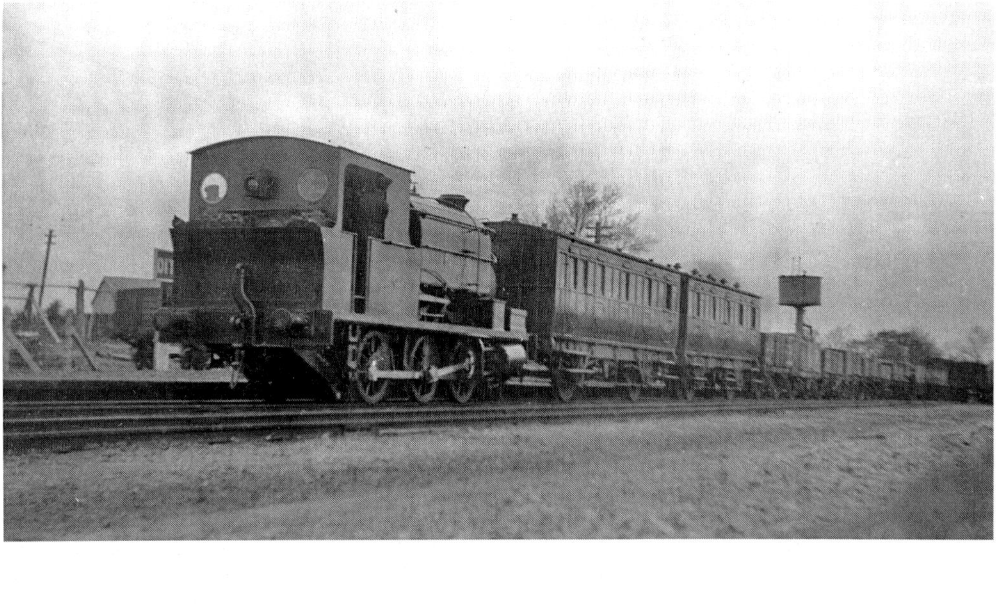

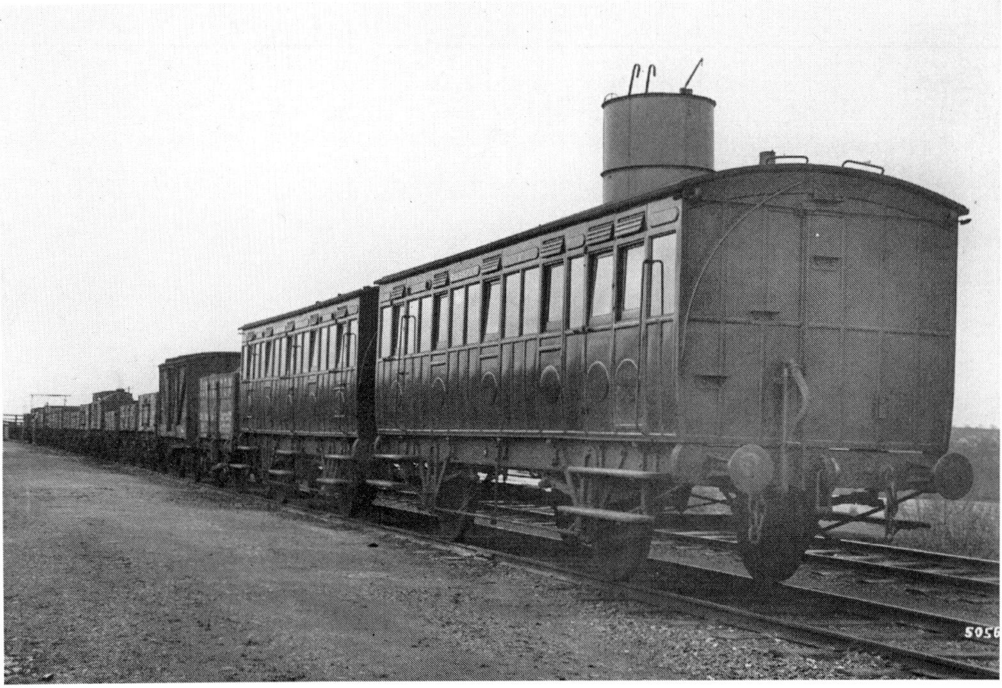

The original ex-North London coaches. *Locomotive Publishing Co./Oakwood Collection*

CM&DP stone wagon at Shipton-under-Wychwood, GWR.
Packer Studios/Centre for Oxfordshire Studies

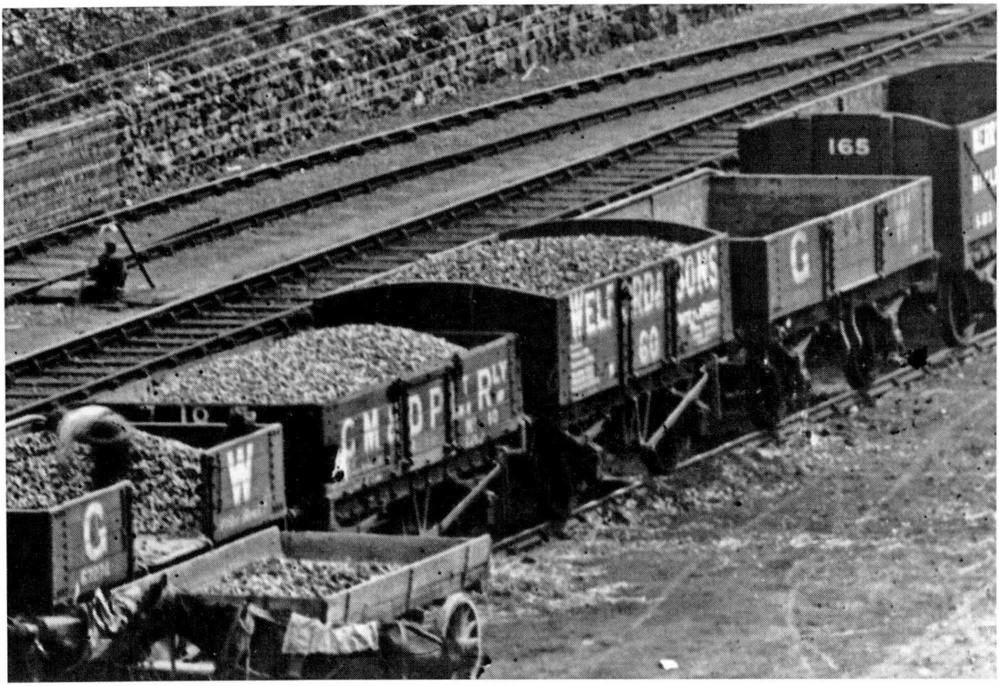

May, 1900.

Cleobury Mortimer & Ditton Priors Light Railway.

ESTIMATE OF THE PROPOSED LIGHT RAILWAY.

Length of Line - 12 miles, 1 furlong, 7 chains. Gauge - 4 feet 8½ inches. Single Line.

No.	Main Heads.	Sub.-Heads.	Cubic Yards.	Price per Yard.	Sub. Heads. Totals.	Sub. Heads. Rate per mile.	Main Heads. Totals.	Main Heads. Rate per mile.
					£	£	£	£
I	Earthworks, Cuttings	Rock ...	20,693	3/-	3103.9			
		Soft Soil..	130,128	1/-	6506.4			
		Roads ...	94	2/6	11.8			
		Total	150,915		9622.1		9622.1	788
II	Embankments, including Roads		131,176	6d.	3279.4		3279.4	268.5
III	Bridges, Public Roads	—			856	70	856	70
IV	Accommodation Bridges and Works ...	—			2368	194	2368	194
V	Viaducts	River Bridges and Viaduct over Corporation Water Main			3315	271.5	3315	271.5
VI	Culverts and Drains	—			839	68.6	839	68.6
VII	Metallings of Roads and cost of Level Crossings	—			691	56.5	691	56.5
VIII	Gatekeepers' houses at Level Crossings ...	None provided			—	—	—	—
IX	Permanent Way (including fencing) ...	(*a*) Permanent Way...			22764	1864		
		(*b*) Ballast			8109.1	664		
		(*c*) Fencing			2149.4	176		
		(*d*) Ditching			390.8	32		
		(*e*) Mile and Gradient Posts			24.4	2		
		(*f*) Check Rails			305.3	25	33743.1	2763
X	Permanent Way for Sidings and cost of Junction	—			6225	509.7	6225	509.7
XI	Stations	(*a*) Stations, Offices and Staff Quarters ...			4390	359.5	—	—
		(*b*) Station Machinery			2565	210	—	—
		(*c*) Workshop and Store Buildings... ...			1050	86	8005	655.5
XII	Electric Telegraph	—			490	40	490	40
XIII	Plant...	(*a*) Engineering Plant			277	22.7	—	—
		(*b*) Wagon and Carriage Plant			50	4.1	—	—
		(*c*) Station and Office Furniture			204	16.7	531	43.6
					—	—	69964.6	5728.9
XIV	Contingencies	20 per cent.			—	—	13992.9	1145.7
XV	Land and Buildings...	(*a*) Land 67a. 1r. 15p.			4040.6	—	83957.5	6874.6
		(*b*) Building			50	—	4090.6	335
		Total cost of 12m. 1f. 7ch. of Railway ...			—	—	88048.1	7209.6
XVI	Rolling Stock	—					None	included.

E. R. CALTHROP, C.E., M. INST. M. E.,
ENGINEER.

Chapter Three

Inspection and Opening

The Inspecting Officer of the CM&DPLR was Lieutenant-Colonel H.A. Yorke, then Assistant Secretary to the railway department of the Board of Trade. His report states that the railway was 12 miles 67 chains long, laid in second-hand flat-bottom track weighing 72 lb. per yard. At the most severe curves support was provided on the inside by wooden blocks dogspiked, like the rails, to the sleepers. There were passing loops at the four stations of Cleobury Town, Stottesdon, Burwarton and Ditton Priors and sidings at four other outlying places which were, along with Cleobury North Crossing, also to be stopping points. The four stations had small wooden shelters, lamps and nameboards, with platforms only one foot high, just as was provided at the other halting places, although they had, on the whole, rather cruder equipment.

The line had eight underbridges or viaducts built of brick on stone abutments, three of which crossed the Rea and the remainder roads or footpaths. There were no overbridges, but some 13 level crossings excluding those minor ones across tracks and pathways. Ten of the 13 were over parish roads and protected only by wooden slat cattle guards, notice and speed restriction boards. These arrangements also applied to an eleventh crossing with a more important road. The other two, at Cleobury Town and Cleobury North Crossing, had fairly substantial gates, but as the latter was some distance from a station with staff it was requested - and subsequently authorised - that the guard or fireman of each train passing might open and close the gates. At the ungated crossings trains had to whistle and keep within a speed limit of 10 mph in case of emergencies, and in foggy or snowy weather linesmen had to place detonators on the track three hundred yards from the various crossings as a warning. Beyond the Wyre Common crossing, at the summit of the 1 in 60 slope down to the junction with the Great Western at Cleobury Mortimer, GWR bound freight trains had to stop to pin down brakes, the locomotive's brake being kept in reserve. Over the same portion passenger trains were restricted to 15 mph.

The actual operation of the railway was relatively simple. The only signal required was a junction distant, fixed at danger, for trains from the light railway arriving at Cleobury Mortimer Junction, but there was also an up home between the CM&DP and the GWR in the short space they were alongside before entering the station, and a down starter for trains from the Great Western onto the railway.

The line was worked on the 'one engine in steam' principle, or by two engines coupled together carrying the train staff: This was round, and painted green, bearing also the inscription 'Cleobury Mortimer and Ditton Priors'. It was without tickets, but single operation was possible. When not required the staff was kept in the station master's office at Cleobury Town, this point also being the headquarters of the railway. The railway was equipped with the telephone throughout.

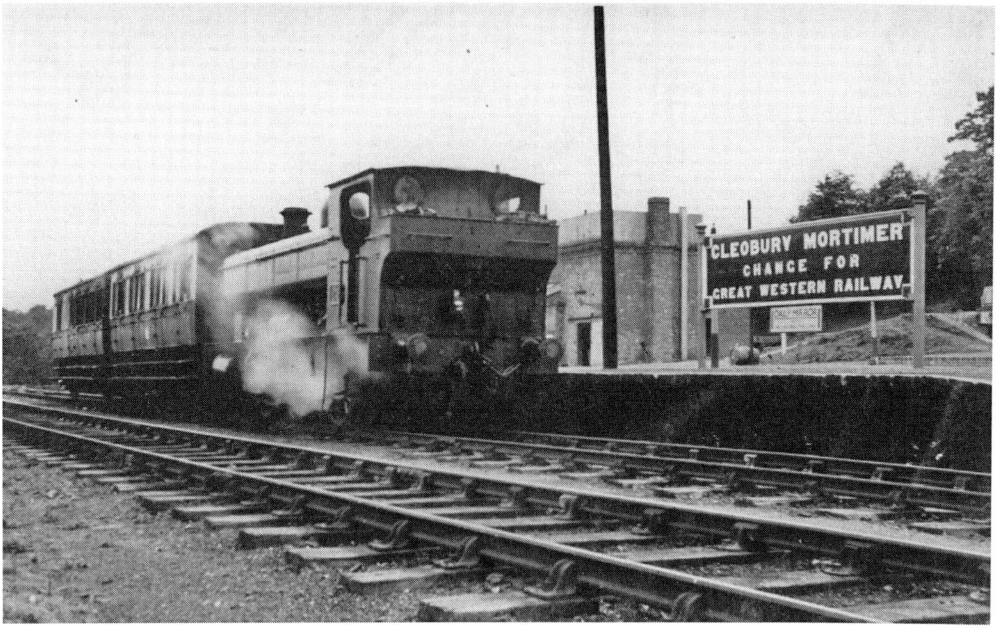

A view of one of the locomotives with its train at Cleobury Mortimer Junction in rebuilt form. The first locomotive to have been rebuilt was No. 29, in 1924. *R.J. Buckley*

Locomotive No. 28 was sent to Swindon works to be rebuilt by the GWR in 1930; it resumed its duties on the line in December 1931. It is seen here at Cleobury Mortimer Junction.

R.E. Tustin

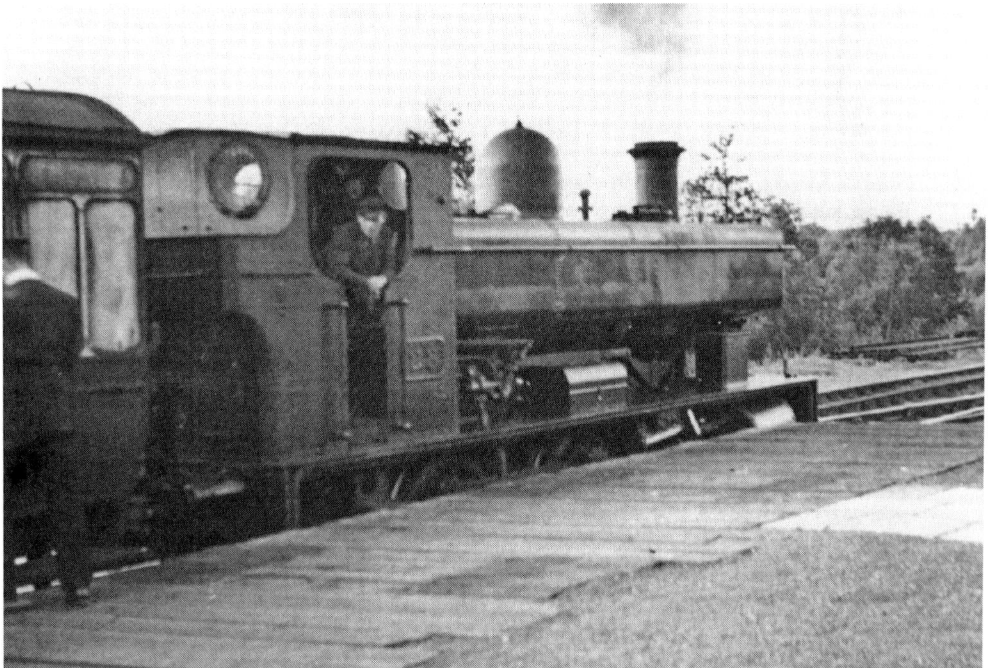

After his inspection, Lieutenant-Colonel Yorke approved the opening of the railway to passenger traffic under certain conditions. The most important of these restricted speed to 20 mph (instead of the usual 25 mph allowed by the Light Railways Act) for the first six months of working in order to permit the road bed to consolidate satisfactorily. He also urged the completion of ballasting as quickly as possible, and ordered that until the track was settled it was to be carefully watched and maintained. The responsibility for this was undertaken by the contractors. It was also stipulated that the siding connections at the stations had to be controlled by the key on the train staff, as was already the case at the outlying sidings. Messrs McKenzie and Holland of Worcester, who had attended to the pointwork on the line, made these alterations at the same rates as for the work originally carried out at the latter places, which were, incidentally, controlled by single lever ground frames. The use of balance levers and padlocks on the points at the stations was also a subject of disapproval, and Annett's locks were consequently fitted.

Accordingly, on 21st November, 1908, (and not 20th November, as originally intended) the CM&DPLR opened to passenger traffic. From Cleobury Mortimer Junction, where the small light railway platform was an exception in being the more usual three feet in height, the route curved away northwards, skirting the Wyre Forest, until almost at right angles to the Great Western line. Once over the summit of the 1 in 60 gradient up to Wyre Common, it was comparatively easy going to Cleobury Town (2 miles). Just before the station, actually at the level crossing, the railway crossed the underground course of the Elan Aqueduct, supplying water from the Elan Reservoir in Wales to Birmingham. When the CM&DP was under construction, the authorities of that city, fearful of local drought, expressed some interest in the well-being of the aqueduct, but all was well. Cleobury Town was so titled in imitation of the practice of other secondary railways, but some would be excused for wondering whether Cleobury Mortimer, pleasant and picturesque as it is, has ever been large enough to really warrant it. On the basis of distance, however, Cleobury Town, being but one mile out of the place, as compared to Cleobury Mortimer Junction's two, was the favourite for the title. Originally it was almost as modest a station as all the others, with the additional feature of a wooden locomotive shed. Later, in World War I, the erection of a reinforced-concrete General Offices building and a locomotive shed in similar material did give the place some air of importance.

From here the railway descended to Chilton Siding (3 miles) and then pursued a constantly curving course, never far from the Rea, to Detton Ford (4½ miles). In March 1908, the CM&DP came to an agreement with the Clee Hill Granite Co., for a connection to sidings serving a stone terminal just north of Detton Ford. This project envisaged the building of an aerial ropeway from the Magpie Quarry on Titterstone Clee Hill to the terminal adjoining the railway. At the time of the Board of Trade inspection this had not been completed, although the work must have been well in hand.

Beyond Detton Ford the line crossed the Rea by a substantial bridge made of local stone and of brick, and continued to Prescott siding (5½ miles). Just north of Prescott the track bridged both the Rea and Farlow Brook by similar

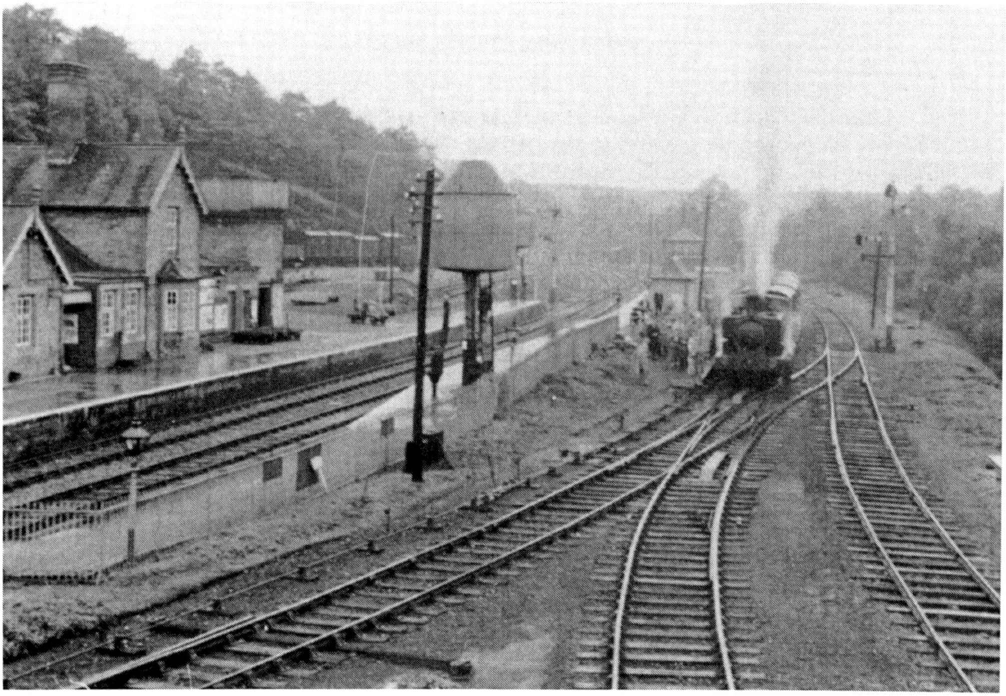

Cleobury Mortimer Junction on 24th September, 1938. The last day of CM&DP passenger service. *D.J. Powell*

No. 28 at the CM&DP platform at Cleobury Mortimer Junction on 11th May, 1938. *N. How Collection*

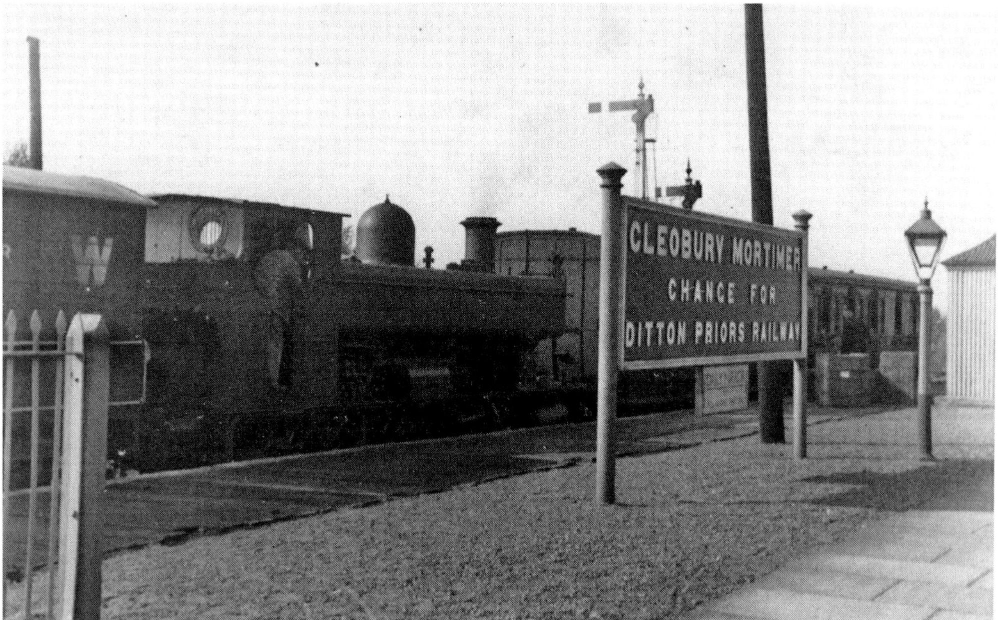

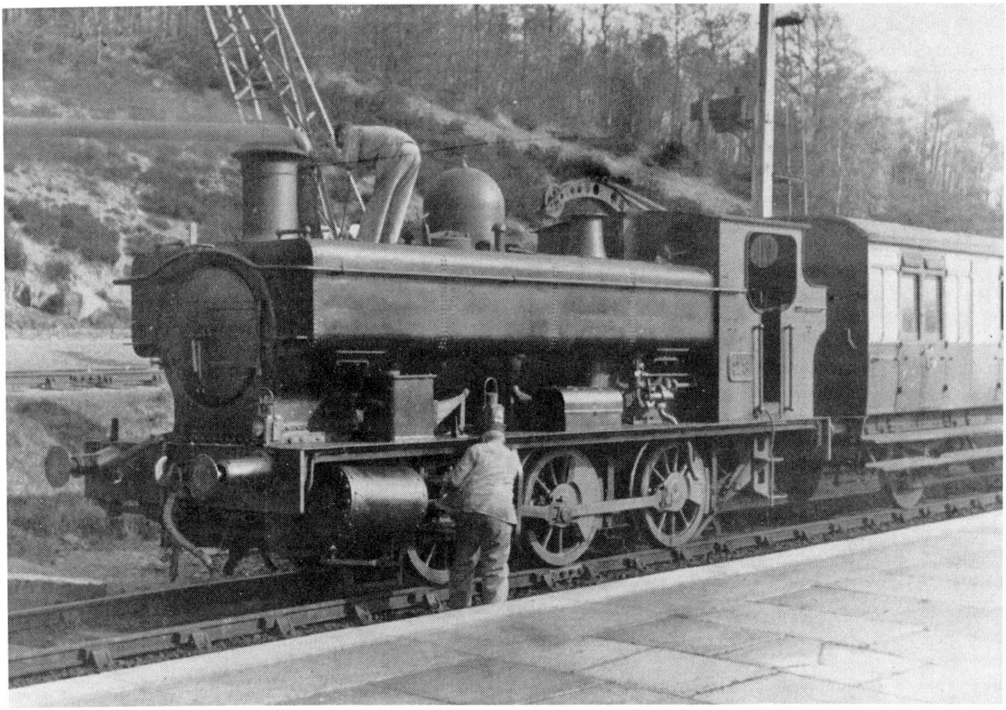

No. 28 takes water at Cleobury Mortimer Junction on 11th May, 1938. *N. How Collection*

No. 29 with a Ditton Priors train at Cleobury Mortimer Junction in 1933.
D.J. Powell/R.S. Carpenter

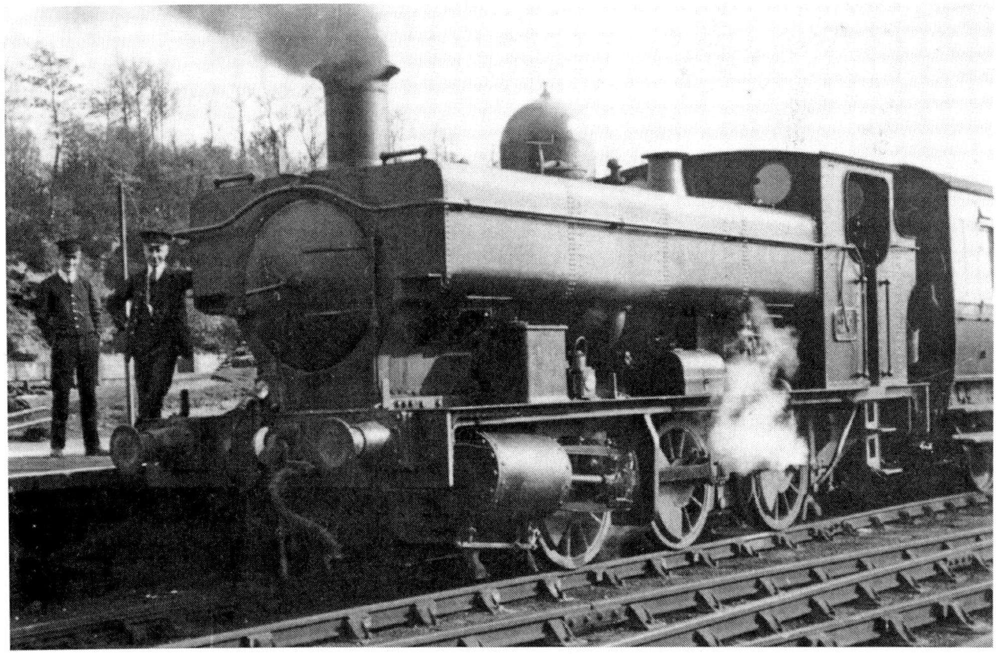

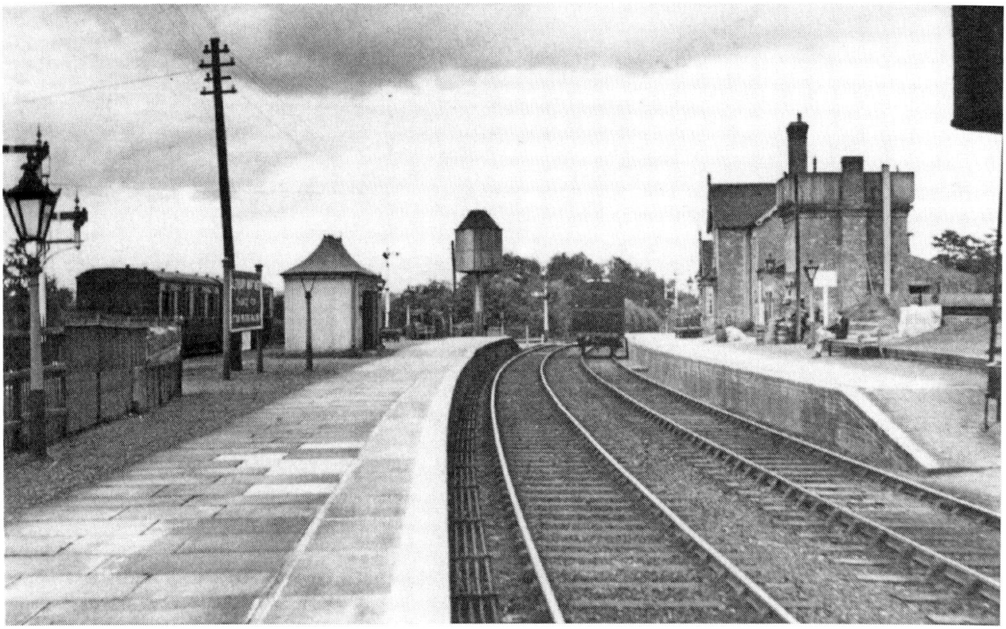

A view of Cleobury Mortimer Junction on 22nd August, 1936. *S.W. Baker*

Pannier tank No. 6430 arrives at Cleobury Mortimer Junction with a train from Bewdley. *W.A. Camwell*

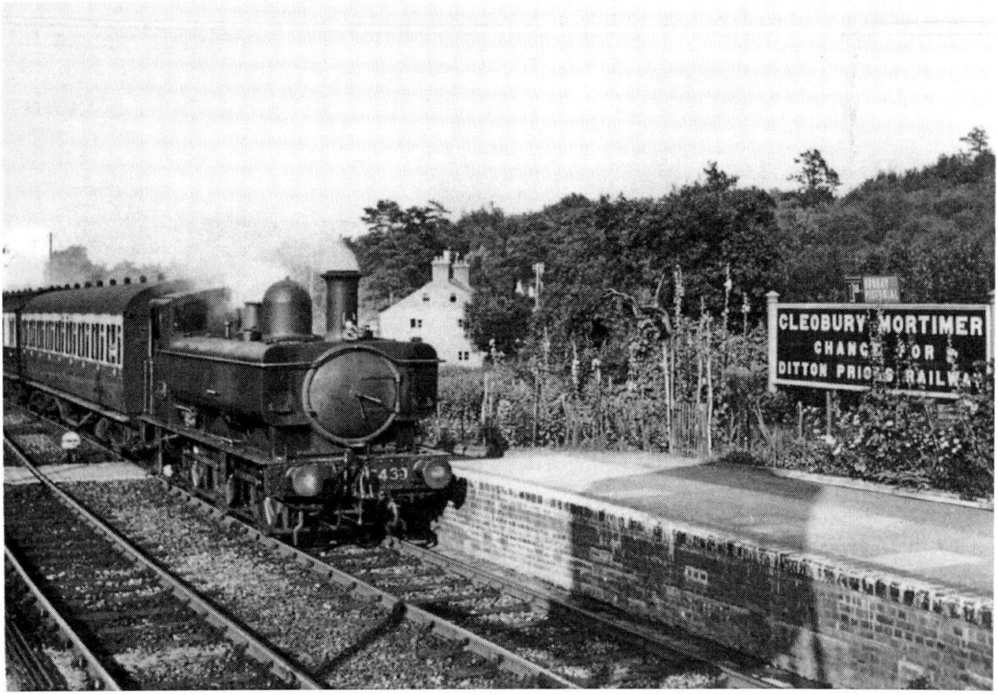

stone and brick bridges before running on up the valley on an adverse gradient to Stottesden (6¾ miles). A short way beyond the route deserted the Rea in favour of its tributary, the Moor Brook, and so came to Aston Botterell Siding (8½ miles), another stopping place blessed with a delightfully rustic name, and Burwarton (9¼ miles), the last intermediate station on the railway. The climb then steepened until Cleobury North Crossing was reached on the last 1 in 60 gradient. It was ironical that, with the possible exception of the terminus, Cleobury North Crossing was the only stopping point at all near the place it was supposed to serve - in fact a somewhat larger community than some of the others - and yet the only such point not granted the dignity of a siding! The last mile and a half from here was largely on the level, and brought the line into Ditton Priors, just 700 ft above sea level. To the west was the dominating outline of the Brown Clee Hill, the source of the railway's early prosperity.

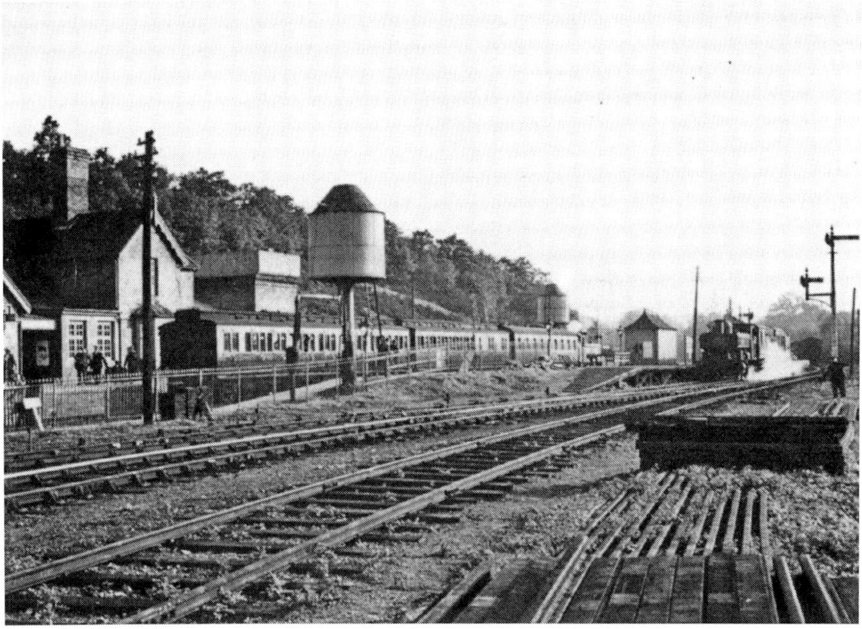

Another view of Cleobury Mortimer Junction with a westbound train headed by GWR pannier tank No. 6430 about to leave. The branch train stands at its platform, headed by one of the rebuilt CM&DPR tank engines. *W.A. Camwell*

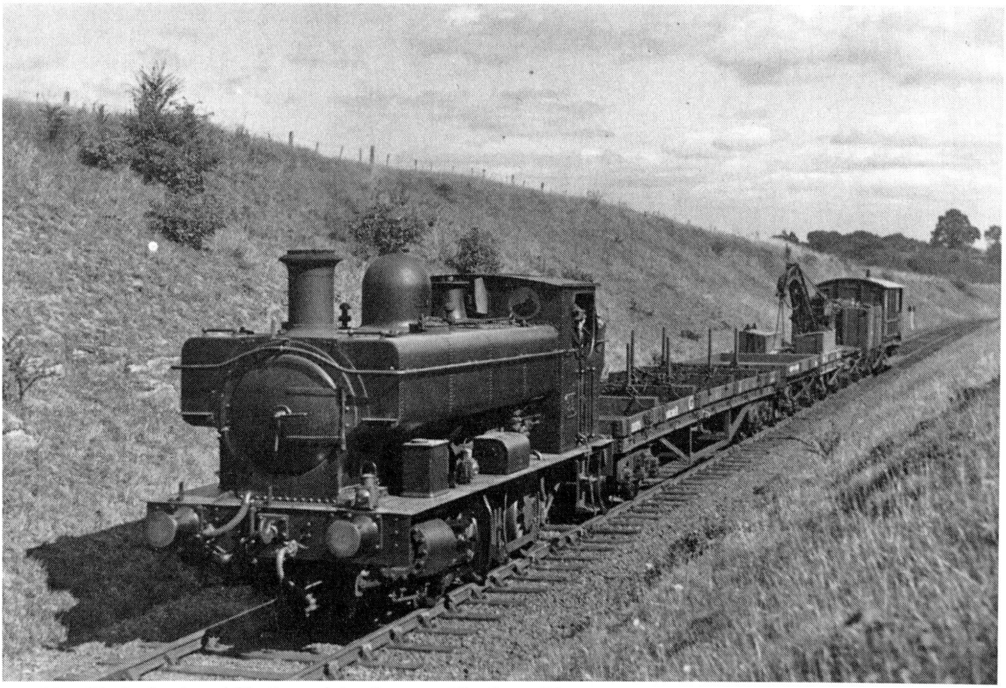

No. 29 climbs from Cleobury Mortimer to Cleobury Town. *N. How Collection*

No. 29 stands at Cleobury Town with railway staff. Guard Ted Teague stands on the far left, and guard W. Futrill near the front of the engine. The two men closest to the locomotive are driver J. How and, in the cab, fireman W. Breakwell.

N. How Collection

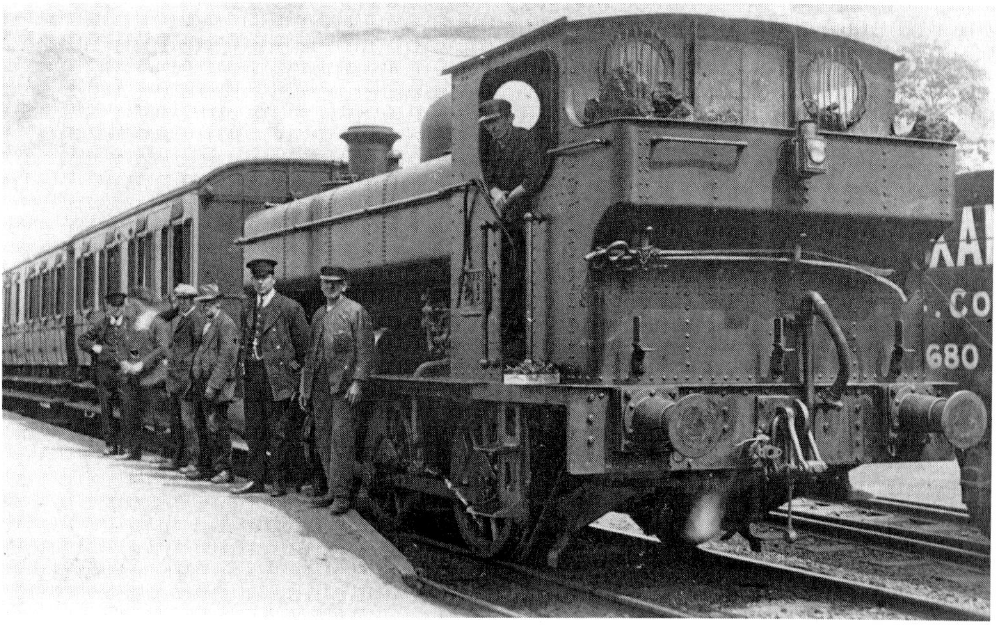

Chapter Four

Locomotives and Rolling Stock

The first locomotives on the CM&DP were those belonging to contractors, Messrs Bott & Stennett. No less than six engines have been reported, and there appears to be no doubt about the use of five of them. The two oldest were by Manning, Wardle & Co. Ltd, being the 0-6-0ST *Trent* (Works No. 626 of 1876) and the 0-6-0ST *Kingswood* (Works No. 729 of 1880). Hudswell, Clarke & Co. were responsible for building the 0-6-0ST *Fleetwood* (Works No. 318 of 1888) and the more modern 0-6-0ST *Lily* (Works No. 621 of 1902). Another Leeds manufacturer, the Hunslet Engine Co. Ltd, produced an 0-4-0ST named *Canada* (No. 525 of 1890). In addition the Hunslet 0-6-0ST *Uxbridge* (No. 761 of 1902) is reputed to have been employed on this contract, but the only photograph seen is a distant view of what looks very like a Manning, Wardle product.

As the construction of the CM&DPLR got under way, the question of locomotives and rolling stock for the company naturally came to the fore. Estimates for a variety of engine types were obtained, of which Mr Foxlee favoured that by Peckett's, costing £1,570 each. His recommendation was largely based on the good reports he had had of similar locomotives operated by Bristol Corporation Docks and the Metropolitan Railway. Nevertheless, the Manning, Wardle design was deemed more suitable, if more costly at £1,970 each, and two were ordered in March 1908. As already mentioned, they did not arrive in time to start the freight service, but were delivered, like the carriages, some days before the opening to passengers. Details of the engines were as follows:

Cleobury
Manning, Wardle 1735/1908: GWR/BR No. 28: Withdrawn 11/1953
Burwarton
Manning, Wardle 1734/1908: GWR/BR No. 29: Withdrawn 2/1954
Pressure: 160 lb.* Driving Wheels: 3 ft 6 in.
Cylinders (two, outside): 16 in. x 22 in.

* *Railway Magazine* April 1909 states 175 lb., but no other evidence is available to this effect, certainly 160 lb. when rebuilt.

As originally built each weighed 30 tons, 11 cwt. empty and 38 tons, 2 cwt. in working order. The water capacity was 870 gallons and the wheelbase a total of 10 ft 6 in. (4 ft 10 in. leading to driving, and 5 ft 8 in. driving to trailing axle), the arrangements being that of an 0-6-0 saddle tank. The locomotive livery was green with black banding, this being edged with red and yellow. The frames, wheels and cylinders were black lined in yellow, and the rectangular nameplates were of brass with a background painted variously vermilion or black. Under the GWR the engines were given numbers, the plates being in the Great Western style. No. 29 was rebuilt as early as 1924 as a pannier tank

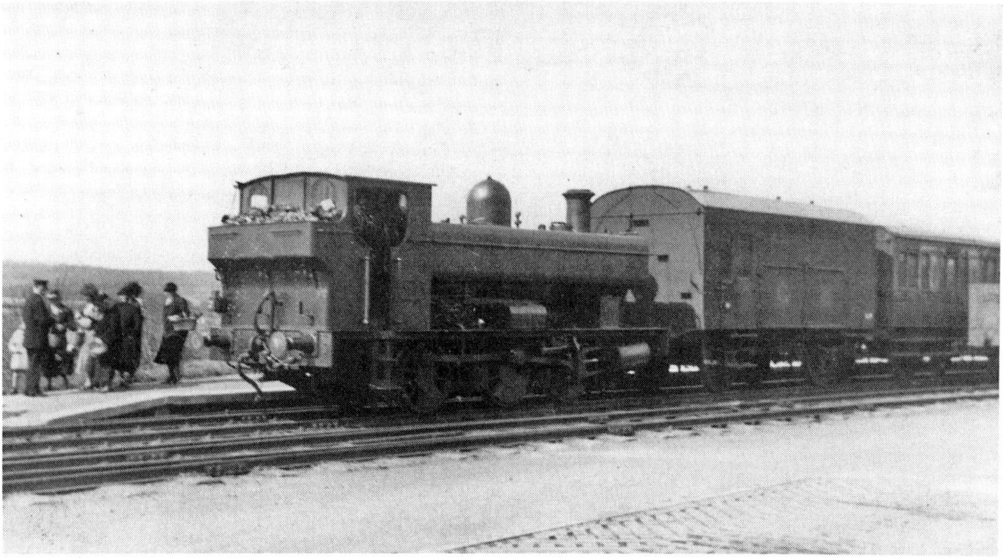

As locomotive No. 29 prepares to leave Cleobury Town for Cleobury Mortimer Junction, passengers can be seen handing in their tickets, 30th March, 1938. *N. How Collection*

Cleobury Town station, 1938. *D.J. Powell/R.S. Carpenter*

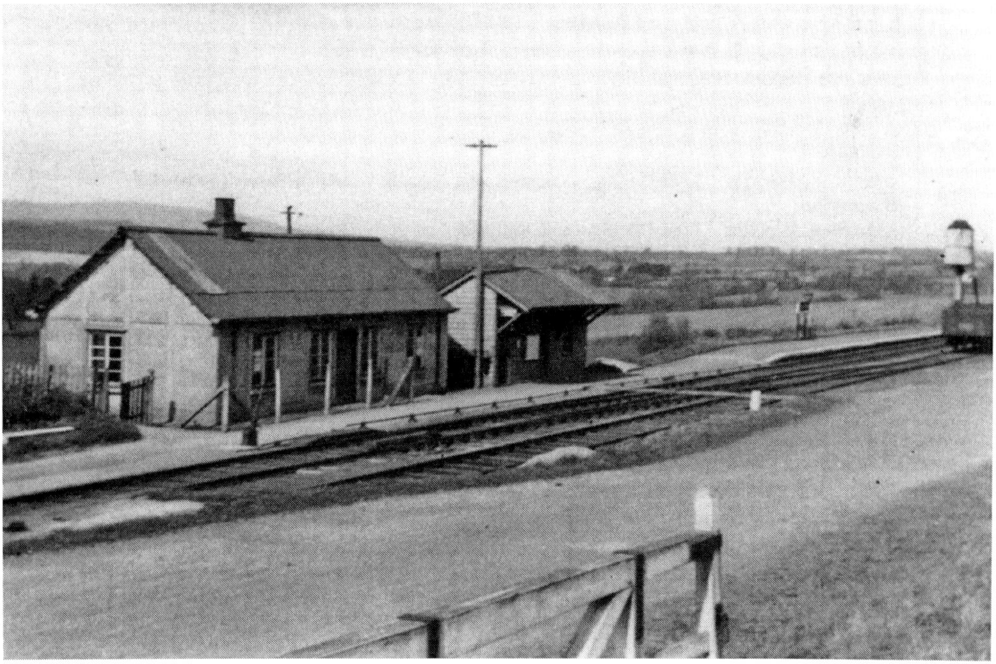

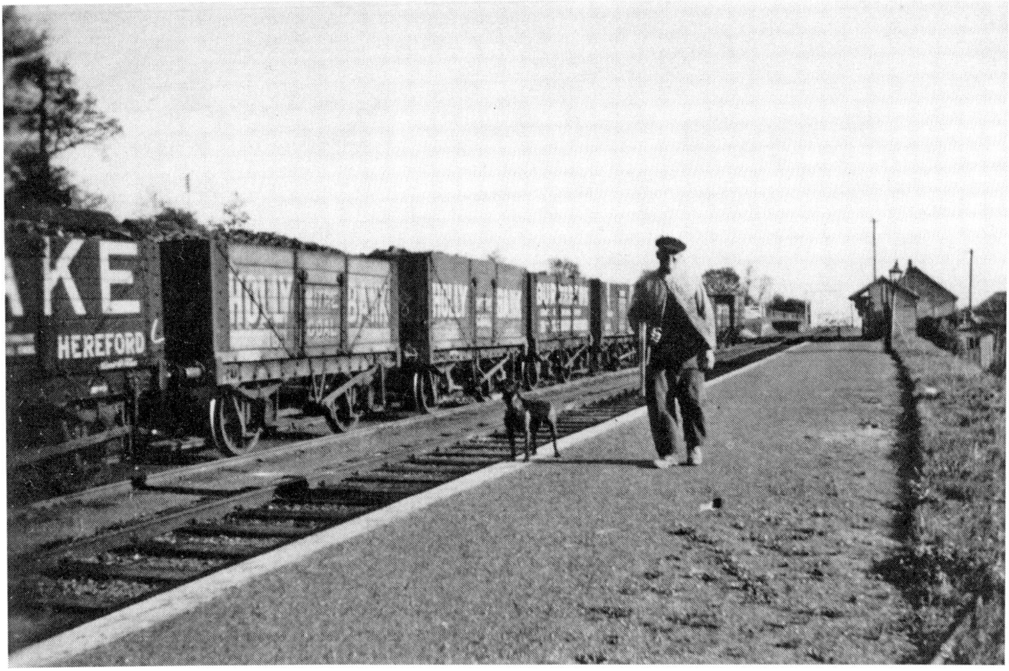

Driver J. How in search of food for the pot, Cleobury Town. *N. How Collection*

Cleobury Town station, view looking north. *Mowat Collection*

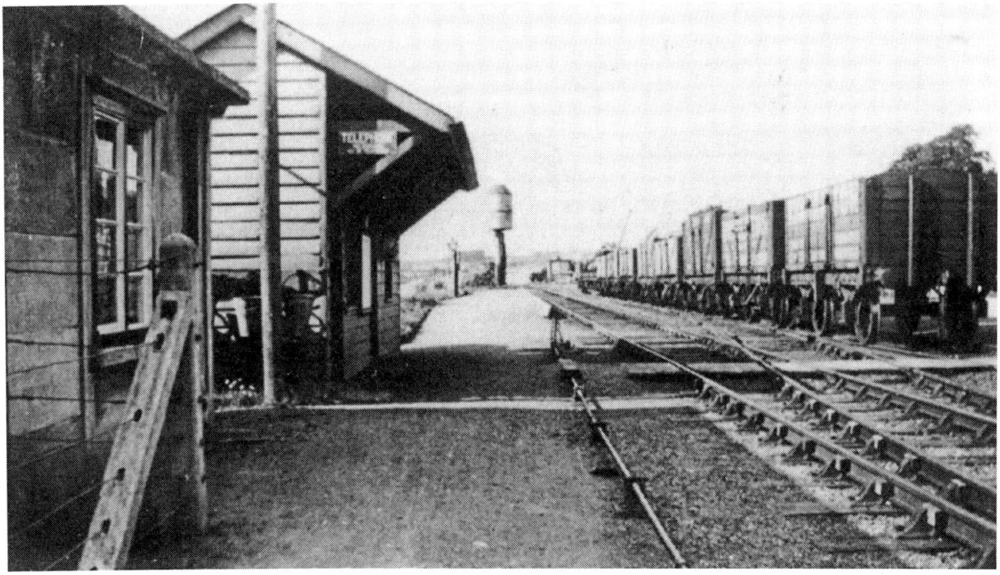

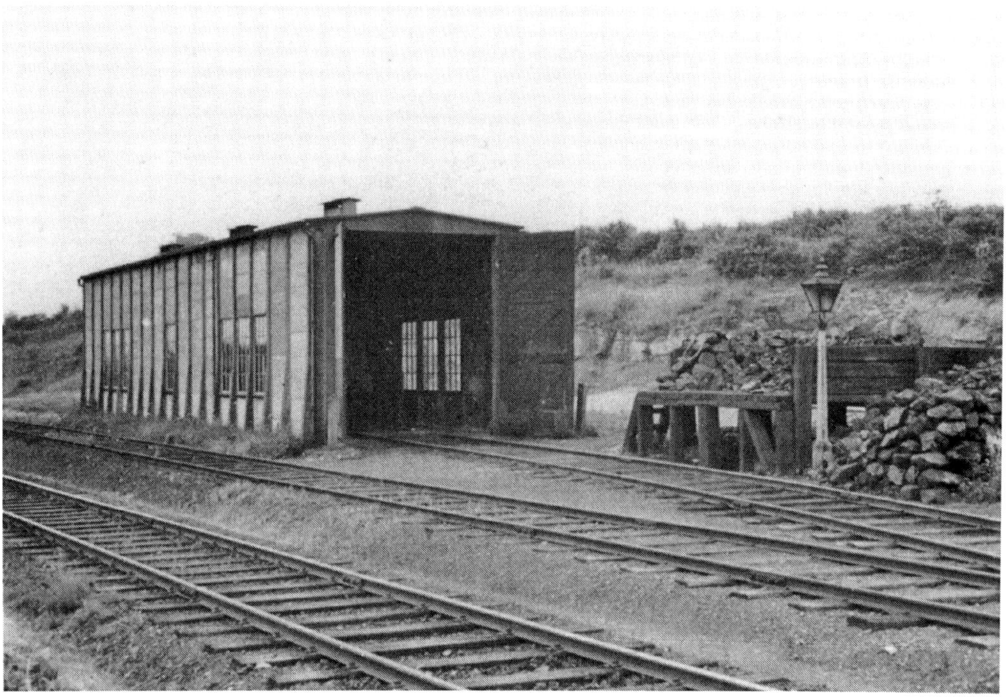

A view of Cleobury Town engine shed *c.* 1938. *W.A. Camwell*

Former Llanelly & Mynydd Mawr Railway locomotive No. 803 at Cleobury Town. *R. Daniells Collection*

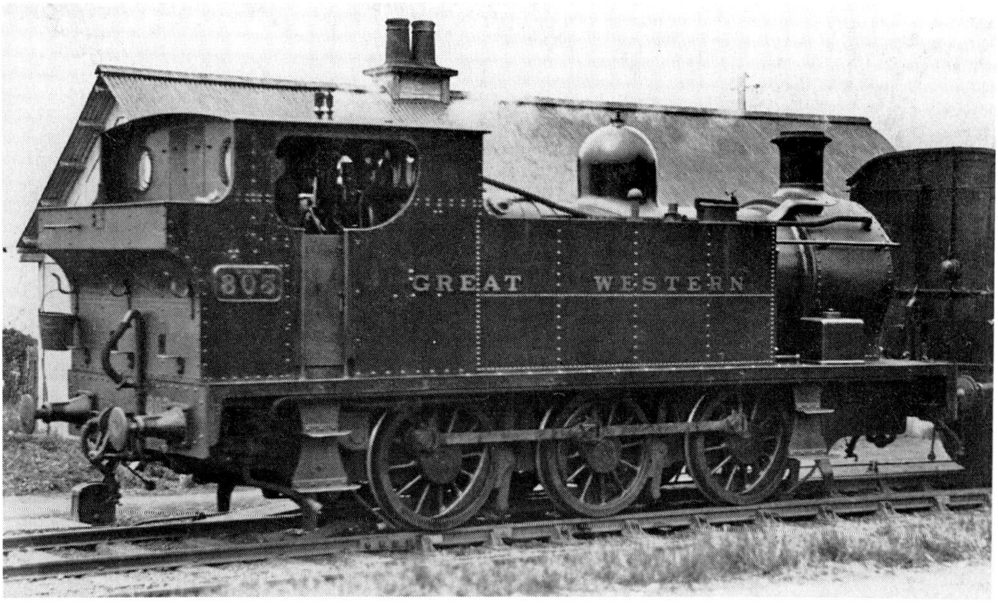

although No. 28 did not go to Swindon for this treatment until September 1930. Evidently the latter was at Swindon for a full 18 months during which time, as will be described, substitute motive power was used on the CM&DP. The nameplates were removed when the saddle-tanks were replaced by panniers. The final rebuilt weight was 39 tons, 18 cwt. and they had a tractive effort of 18,235 lb.

Prior to rebuilding however, in early operation on the CM&DPLR, some minor mechanical difficulties were encountered, the most serious being the tendency of *Burwarton* to run hot. Simple repair jobs were well within the capacity of the depot at Cleobury Town, although major overhauls had to be undertaken at the Worcester works of the GWR. Once these teething troubles were overcome, it appears that the two locomotives gave most satisfactory service. Indeed, Mr T.R. Perkins, who visited the railway towards the end of its independent existence, records that they were more powerful engines than on many light railways with which he was acquainted, and could easily handle trains of 20 loaded stone wagons. Needless to say, after reconstruction they lost much of their individual character, but continued a rather unremarkable career on the line through Great Western days. Their livery of unlined black, relieved only by the letters 'GWR' on the panniers, was an undistinguished guise in comparison with their former smart appearance; it seems very doubtful whether either engine ever carried British Railways colours, although they survived almost six years on the nationalised system. Some years previous to withdrawal No. 29 acquired one of the ugly 'balloon stack' type spark arresters, and in such condition was probably more active than No. 28, which, having been made surplus in 1949, spent quite a time in store at Kidderminster. It was allowed one last fling shortly before scrapping, when it was dispatched to Newport, apparently for some sort of trials, but both locomotives soon went.

The Grouping also brought about the disappearance of the original coaching stock, which was by that time getting a little elderly. The four vehicles were purchased from the North London Railway for £65 each, £25 being required for the alterations and repairs necessary. Six-wheel stock was prohibited from the CM&DP and, in consequence, they were all four-wheel, and stated at the time to be in good condition. Like the locomotives they were fitted with the vacuum brake. After modification they differed externally from their original condition in a variety of ways. The old buffers were replaced, and the window-bars removed; the footboards were also scrapped, and exchanged for two steps per carriage door, chiefly to suit the lower platforms. According to Lieutenant-Colonel Yorke, incidentally, the steps were not in position at the time of his inspection and he was not able to judge whether or not they would be satisfactory. But the most important feature was the centre corridor the whole length of each carriage, and the doors at the end to enable the guard to pass from one to the other to issue tickets whilst the train was in motion. There were no 'bellows', merely platforms and hand supports. It was, no doubt, quite an enlivening experience to cross from one vehicle to another when rattling down one of the 1 in 60 gradients, although the speed in theory could not, of course, exceed 25 mph.

On the NLR these vehicles had carried carriage numbers 1033, 1034, 1041

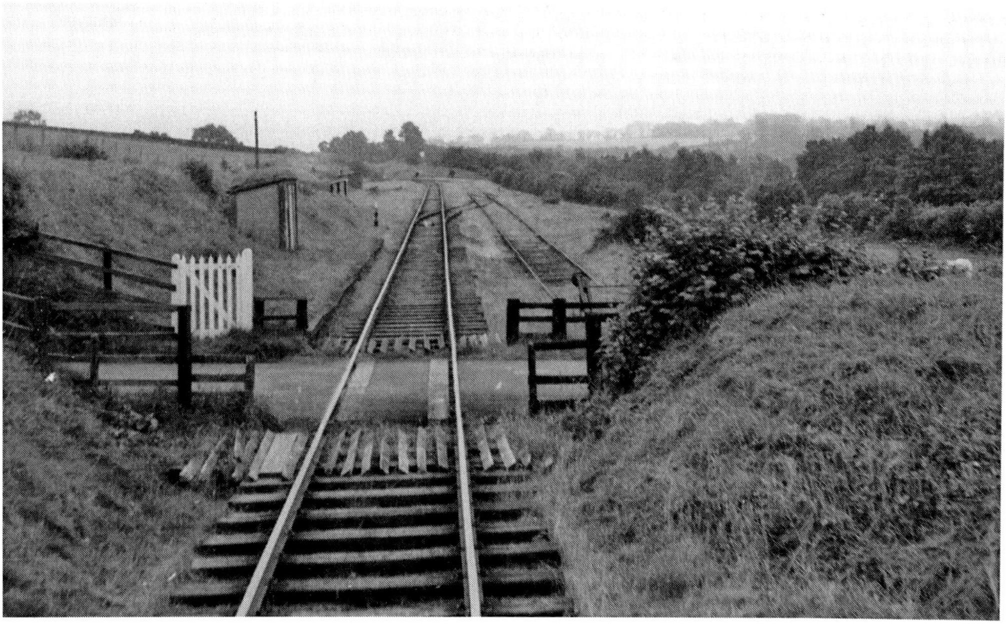

Detton Ford, 1962, showing the goods loop provided for stone traffic. The Catherton Sidings were laid at a slightly lower level, behind the grassy bank on the right. *M.R.C. Price*

Detton Ford on 30th March, 1938, showing the low platform and basic shelter. Amazingly this structure was still in existence 80 years later. *R.K. Cope*

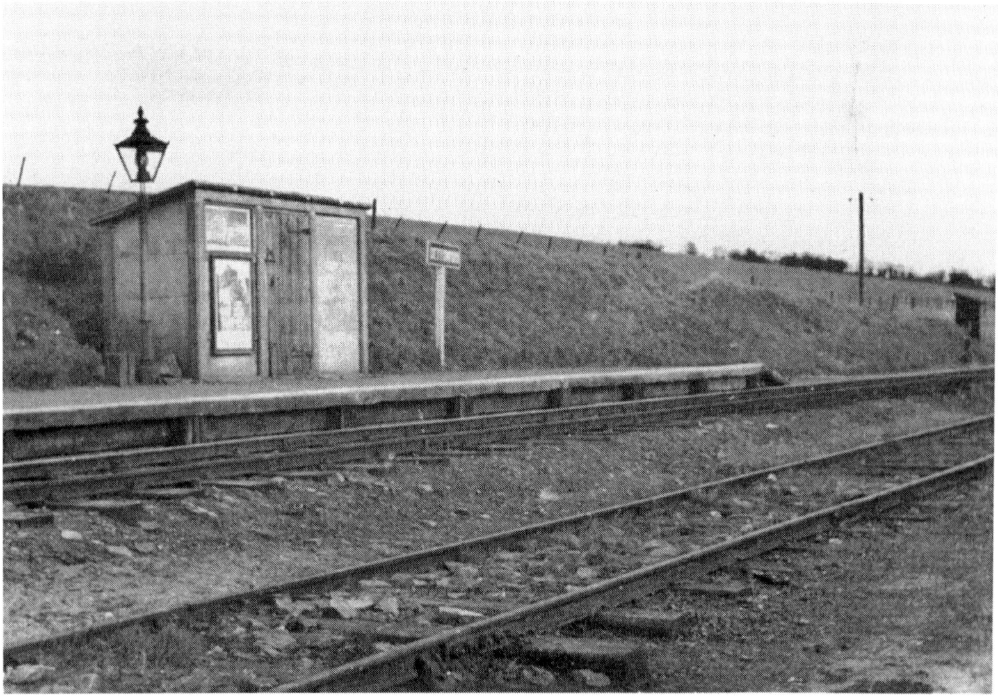

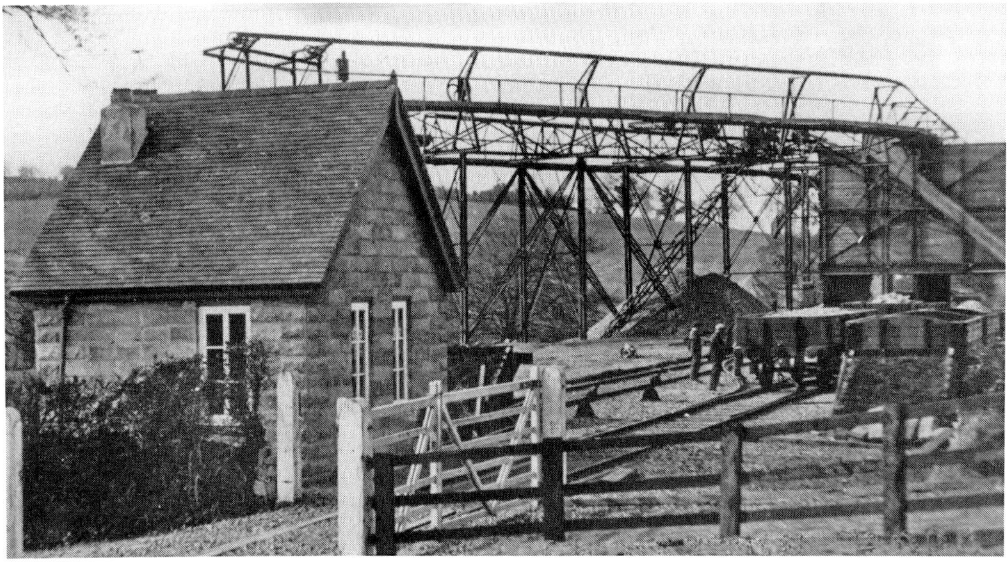

Detton Ford Catherton Sidings *c.* 1914. Within the sidings, wagons were moved by a shunting horse. *R.W. Kidner Collection*

The terminus of the Clee Hill aerial ropeway, Catherton Sidings, 30th March, 1938. *D.J. Powell/R.S. Carpenter*

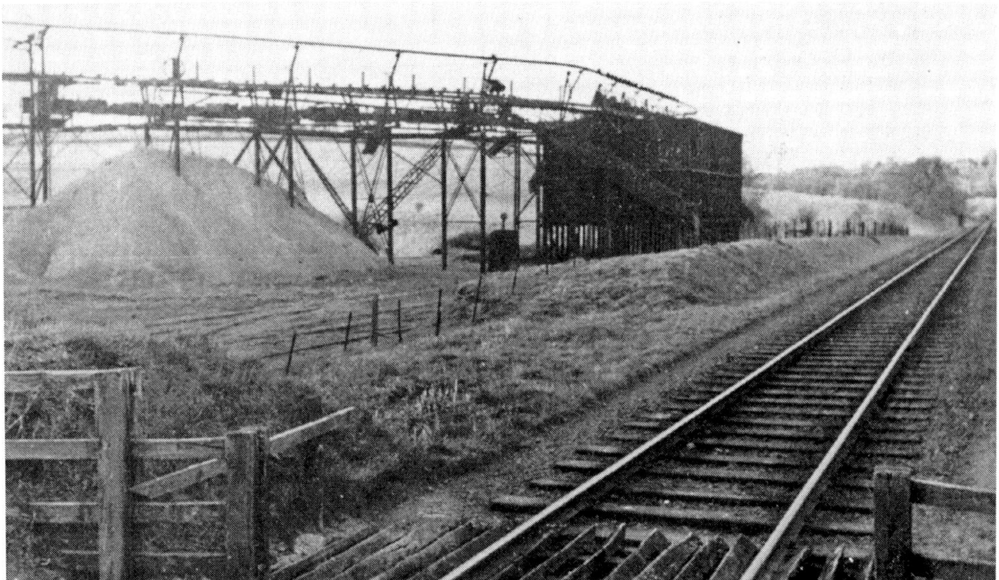

and 1043, but the exact renumbering on the CM&DP is not certain. Suffice to say that CM&DP Nos. 2 and 4 were five compartment 1st/3rd composite coaches. The 1st class was in the centre, and each compartment seated eight. The other two were 3rd class, with three eight-person compartments, also including a brake portion. The livery was initially teak, but was later of the standard Great Western type. In addition to the numeral of the class on the carriage door, the appropriate word was also written out in full in a panel just beneath the door window. On the composite coaches, above the level of the windows, and to the immediate left of the first-class compartment was inserted 'C.M.D.P. Ry', and to the right was the coach number. All four vehicles were 28 ft long on a 15 ft wheelbase.

The GWR replacement stock was also of the four-wheel variety, two being four-compartment coaches, and two longer three-compartment brake vehicles. These were gas-lit and fitted with the vacuum brake.

Ten open 10-ton wagons constituted the first freight stock, these having been obtained from the British Wagon Co. of Rotherham on hire purchase over seven years. They also supplied two four-wheel brake vans, of 10 ft wheelbase, on a similar basis. Weighing 19½ tons tare each, these had been specially built and equipped to control the heavy stone trains on the severe gradients. The company owned in addition a five-ton travelling crane, which in service found a variety of uses, not least being to move stone and timber. In 1909 a crane wagon was obtained to accompany this. In 1912 the goods stock, which had a livery of grey, was further supplemented by ten 8-ton open wagons (Nos. 11-20), made necessary by the expanding traffic on the CM&DPLR. An element of uncertainty over the capacity of these wagons has persisted because their dimensions (14 ft 7 in. x 6 ft 11 in. x 2 ft 4 in.) were almost identical to those of the earlier wagons said to be of 10 ton capacity. Although the point was queried at the time, these weight designations remained. The Abdon Clee Stone Quarry Co. also bought a batch of similar wagons from the British Wagon Co. In addition, the Clee Hill Granite Co. had its own wagons for traffic to and from Detton Ford, whilst the Burwarton Coal & Trading Co. also had private owner wagons for traffic to Ditton Priors and Cleobury Town, as well as Burwarton.

With the absorption of the railway into the Great Western the entire collection of locomotives and rolling stock passed into the hands of the main line company with the exception of one wagon damaged beyond repair in 1920. The GWR was not impressed with most of its acquisitions, and almost all the 8-ton vehicles were withdrawn without ever carrying their new numbers. The original 10-ton wagons, plus No. 11 - redesignated as having 10-ton capacity - were given new numbers between 34238 and 34268. The last two, Nos. 7 and 8 on the CM&DP were withdrawn in 1928. The brake vans did better, the former No. 1 lasting until 1936, and the former No. 2 until 1932. The carriages, on the other hand, did not last long, being withdrawn in 1925 and 1926, although the body of one of the brake thirds was sold for private use.

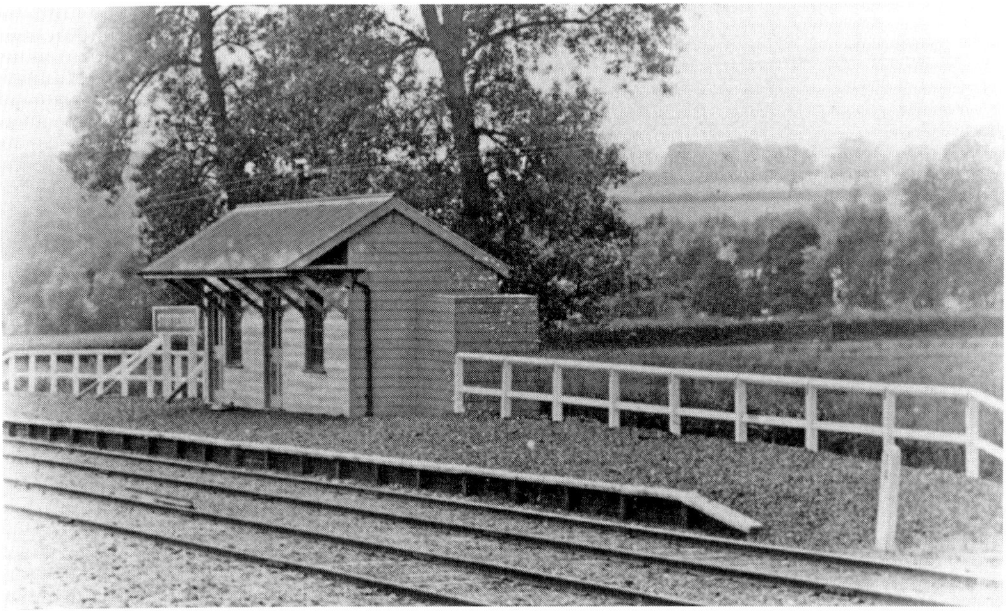

A 1908 view of Stottesden station. By 1910 the spelling of the station name had been changed to Stottesdon. *R.C. Riley Collection*

Stottesdon station, from the south. *Nelson Collection*

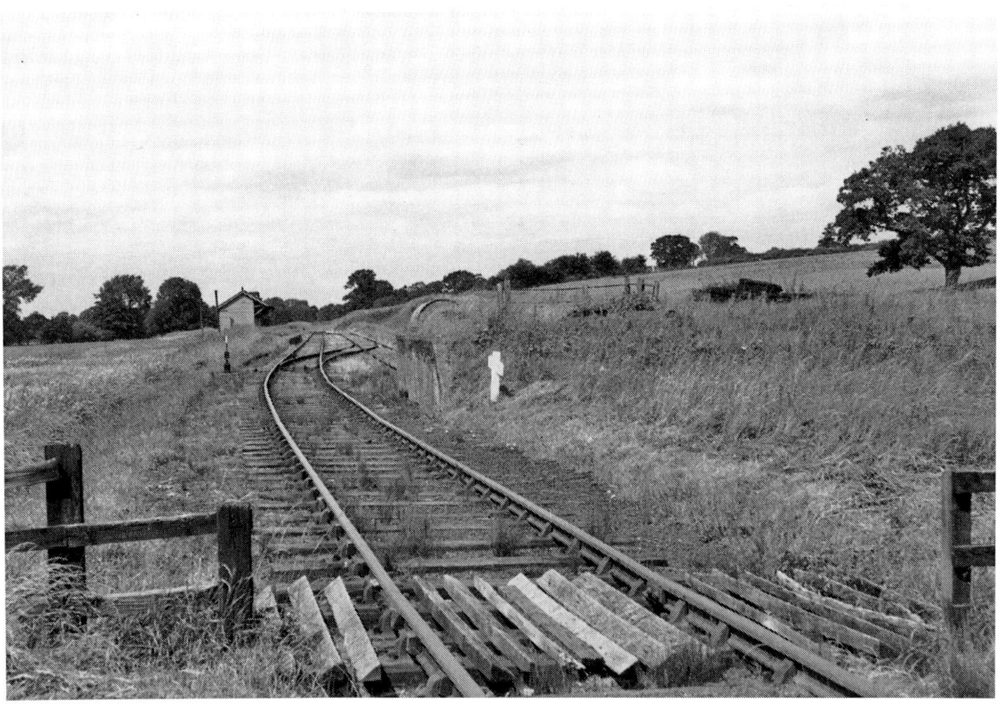

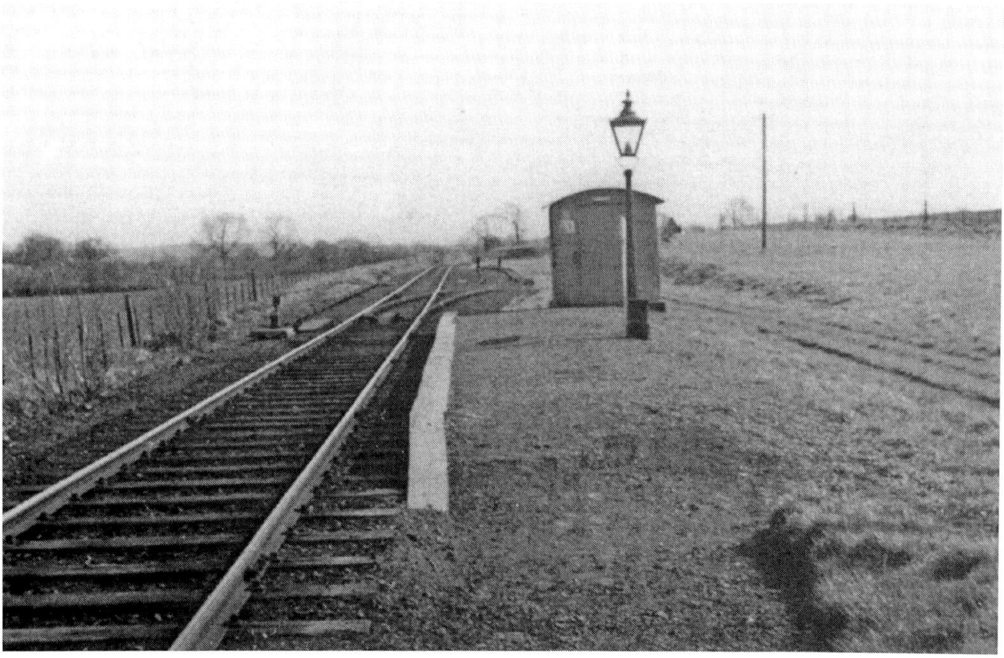

Aston Botterell Siding, viewed looking south, 1938. *D.J. Powell/R.S. Carpenter*

The site of Aston Botterell Siding, August 1975. *Author*

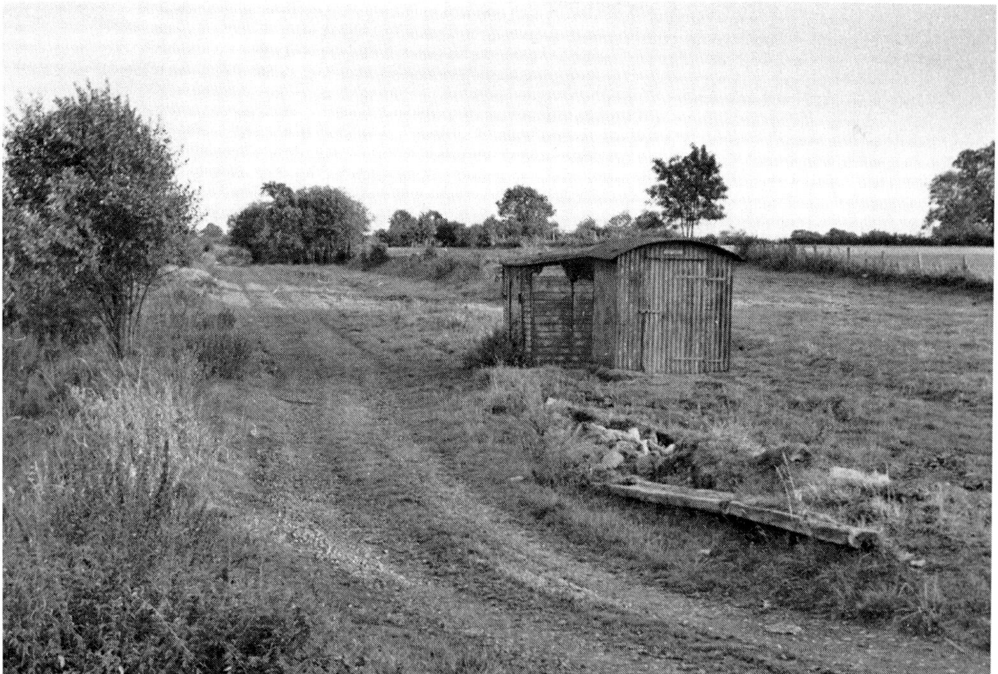

Chapter Five

Independent Operation

Almost immediately the railway was opened it began to show the promise originally forecast by its promoters. Quite apart from the fact that this vindicated their faith in their concern, its development through its independent days must have been most satisfying. How many minor lines, after all, failed to live up to the ambitious and over-optimistic expectations of their supporters? In this case they could thank themselves that they had selected as Manager so able and energetic a man as Mr E.J. Morris, who had from boyhood been in railway service. He began in April 1876 as a ticket sorter on the Metropolitan Railway, and subsequently rose through the ranks of booking clerk and relief clerk to become a station master at Wembley Park and then later at Neasden. Prior to his appointment to the CM&DPLR in May 1908, he was a goods canvasser, and afterwards an outdoor representative of that department of the Metropolitan. On the light railway he organised all the traffic working, and was largely responsible for improving the resources of the district and the CM&DP's capacity to satisfy its needs. His activity was further reflected in the neat and well maintained condition of the line and its equipment.

By 1909 the CM&DPLR was firmly established, for in this, the first complete year of operation, a profit of some £734 on a revenue of £3,370 was made. A total of 17,240 train miles were run, 286 being passenger, 602 freight and the remainder mixed. This thriving state of affairs not only lasted, but continued to improve, as is shown by the figures for the company up to the start of World War I. The operating surpluses for the years 1910, 1911 and 1912 were £1,003, £2,214 and £2,325 respectively; in 1913 this rose to £3,052 from an income of £6,450 (£5,912 from freight) and expenses of £3,398, although the total locomotive mileage stayed at a constant 19,066.

So much for statistics; the reason for the prosperity lay, as already pointed out, in the mineral traffic emanating from Ditton Priors and also Detton Ford. At this latter point, in February 1909, the aerial ropeway opened to connect it with Magpie Quarries on the Titterstone Clee Hill, in the workings of which was a small narrow gauge tramway. The stone, similar to that found elsewhere in the Clee Hills, was simply taken down to Detton Ford in buckets which then returned empty up the other length of the endless rope. The course of the ropeway, which was, for the most part, supported on lattice structures, was via the hamlet of Catherton - hence the stone sidings at Detton Ford were sometimes called the 'Catherton sidings'.

In addition the possibility of having coal traffic over the railway was not forgotten. Although the early scheme under the grandiose title of the Stottesdon, Kinlet and Billingsley Railway, came to nothing, the CM&DP Board was still interested in the possibility of extending north or north-east to the GWR or the LNWR in the industrial area around Coalbrookdale.

It was recognised that northern continuation of the CM&DPLR from Ditton Priors would also provide a second outlet for the railway to facilitate the

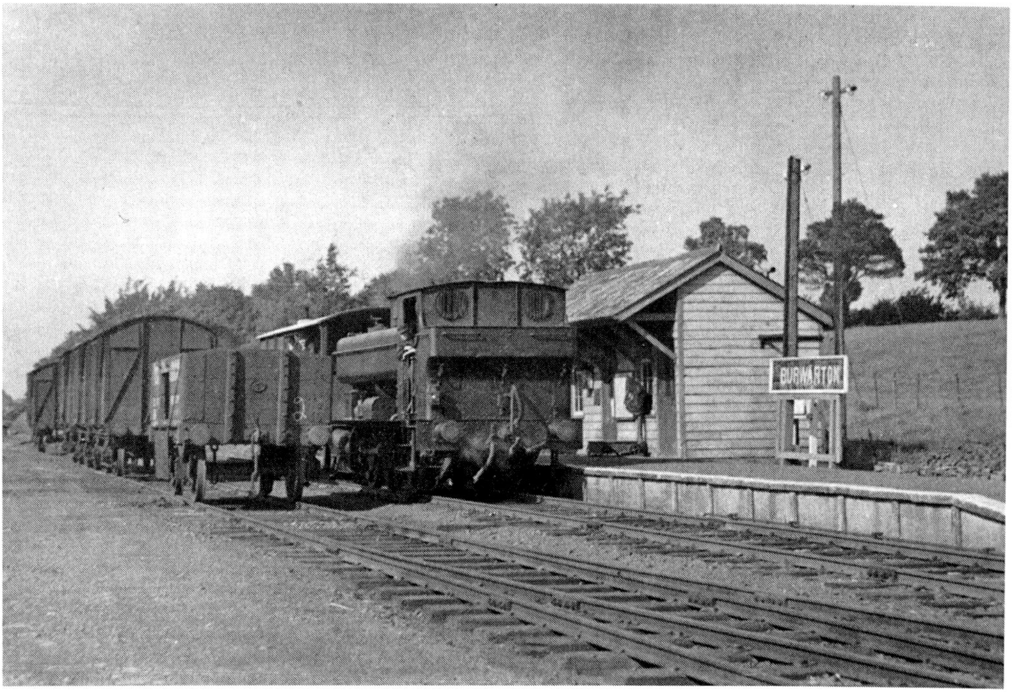

No. 29 and brakevan pause at Burwarton, *c.* 1936. *N. How Collection*

Burwarton station on 30th March, 1938. *D.J. Powell/R.S. Carpenter*

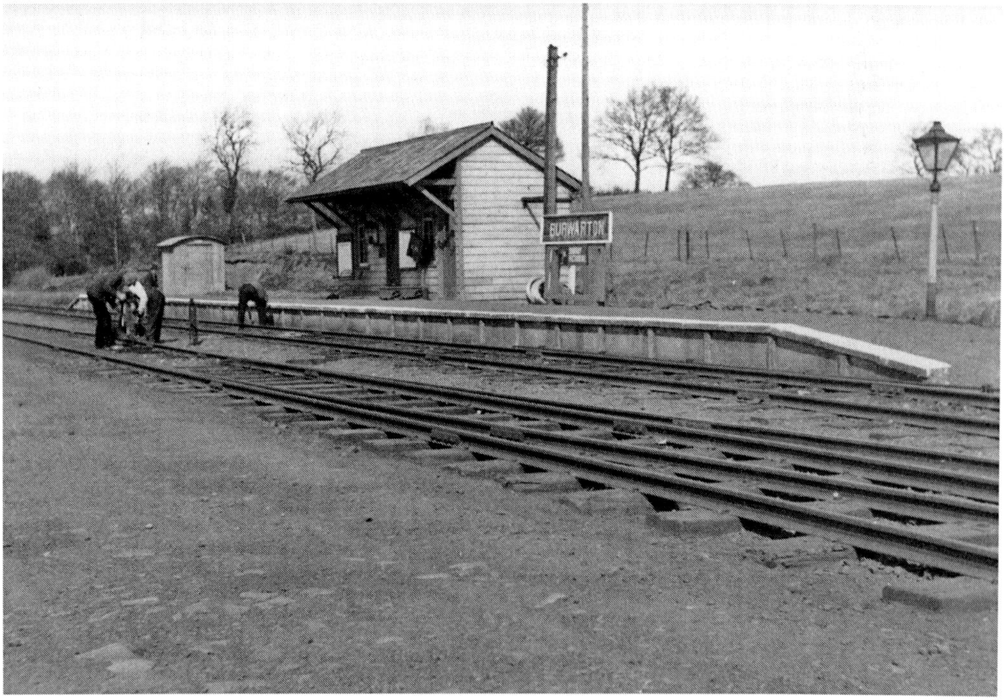

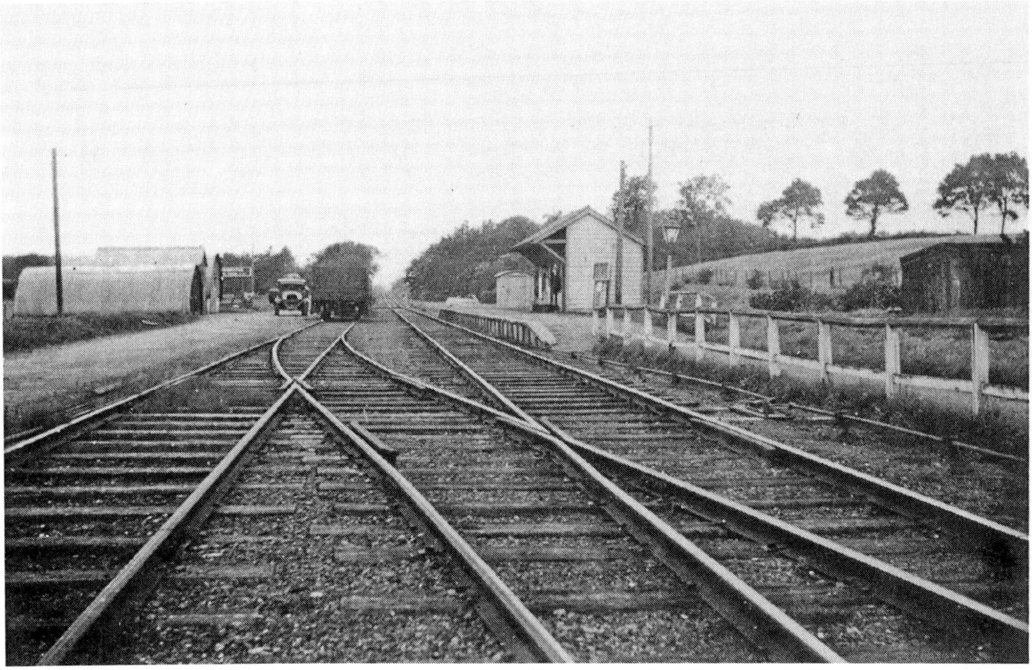

Burwarton station from the south. On the left can be seen the buildings of the Burwarton Coal & Trading Co. *Mowat Collection*

Burwarton station site, 1992. Note the platform edge still in position. *Author*

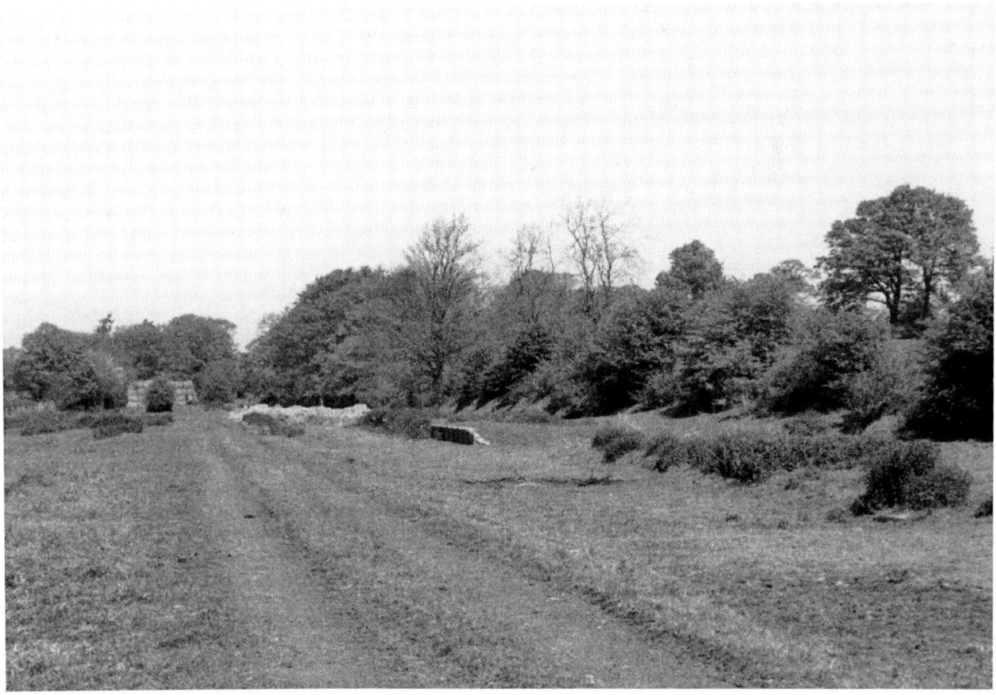

flourishing stone traffic, and enable it to serve the rich agricultural area of Corve Dale, between the Clee Hills and the Wenlock Edge. Mr Foxlee, writing to Mr Stennett of the contractors on 16th February, 1912, said there were three possible extensions, namely:

(1) A north-easterly line to the GWR Severn Valley Branch, a distance of eight miles. It would involve severe gradients and cost about £7,500 per mile.

(2) A continuation to the London and North Western Railway at Coalport, some 12 miles, and having very heavy works and steep gradients. The cost would be £8,000-£10,000 a mile or a prohibitive total of £96,000-£120,000.

(3) A northward extension from Ditton Priors, running on the surface for 1½ miles and then dipping down into Corve Dale with a station near Weston on the Craven Arms - Bridgnorth road. From here it would have a 1 in 60 gradient, almost on the surface, up to the Much Wenlock branch at Presthope, 200 feet above Corve Dale. The line, 6 miles long, would be cheaply built (a total of £32,500 being necessary), and would have a ruling gradient northwards of 1 in 60 and southwards of 1 in 50.

Mr Foxlee was wholeheartedly in favour of the third proposal, partly because it would best meet the requirements of the locality, and partly from the point of view of economy. His conviction that it would be wholly acceptable to the Directors of the CM&DPLR seems to have been less well founded, however, for there was some hesitation. But evidently what really killed it, like many another extension scheme, was the First World War.

When the CM&DPLR opened the timetable advertised three trains a day each way, all mixed, and to be supplemented by a special service as required. Some 68 or 70 minutes were allowed for the journey of 12 miles. Northbound trains left Cleobury Town at 8.20 am and Cleobury Mortimer Junction at 11.10 am and 4.35 pm the return workings being at 9.35 am, 3.0 pm and 6.5 pm. Such was the development of the freight traffic, however that this service soon had to be curtailed to one in each direction morning and afternoon. Even then, as far as passengers were concerned, on Mondays only the morning train operated, and on Tuesdays and Thursdays the service was suspended altogether! By now, according to T.R. Perkins, the timings had been increased to 78 minutes up to Ditton Priors and 77 back. Meanwhile up to four goods trains a day might be operated to clear the accumulated stone wagons from the railway, and a considerable traffic had also developed in agricultural produce, stone ballast (largely for GWR track) and cement (for a reinforced concrete block works at Ditton Priors). At this time, in the case of the afternoon passenger train, it was customary to terminate at Cleobury Town as the connection at Cleobury Mortimer Junction with the last GWR train to Kidderminster was considered too close to be at all reliable. Nevertheless, it is understood that if there was a passenger intending to make the change, speed, such as was possible, would be applied in the hope of reaching Cleobury Mortimer Junction in time. Whatever the outcome, such occasions provided a fine illustration of public

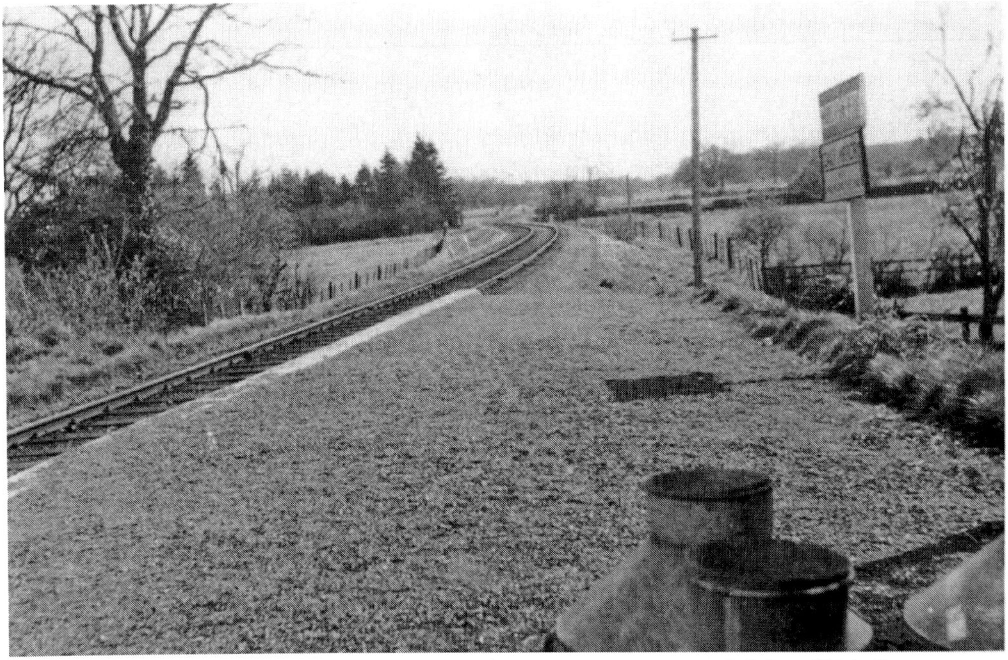

View looking south from Cleobury North Halt. *D.J. Powell/R.S. Carpenter*

Cleobury North Halt and level crossing. The small hut was similar to the shelter at Detton Ford. *Mowat Collection*

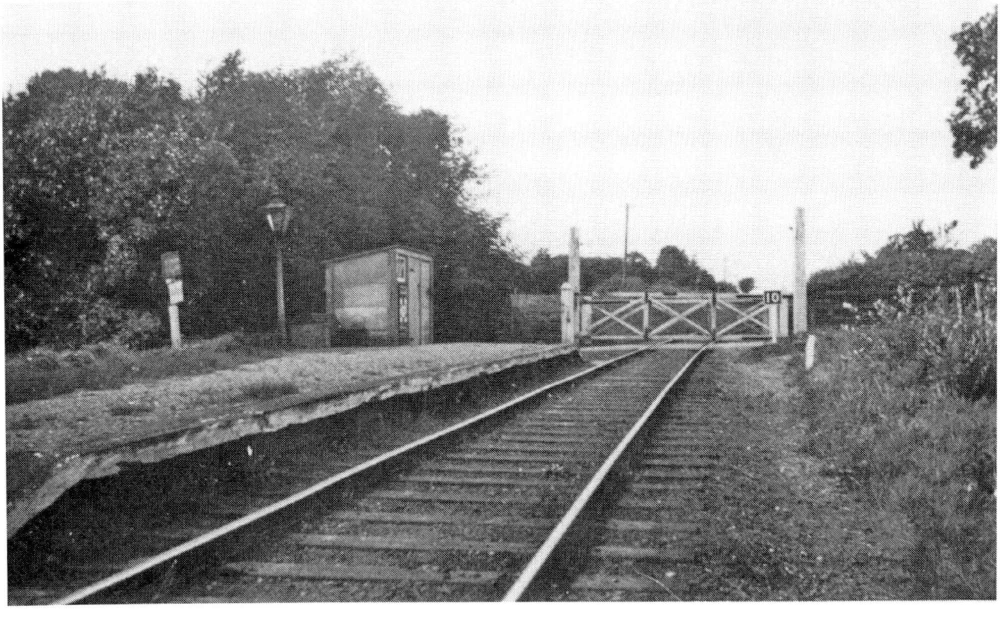

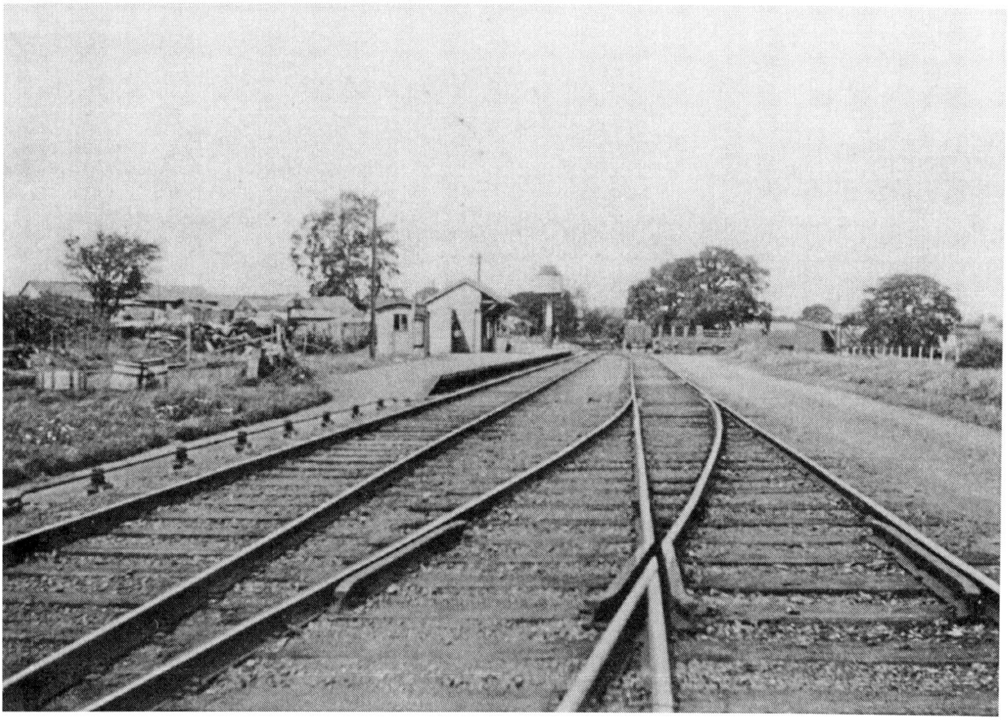

Ditton Priors station looking towards buffer stops. *Mowat Collection*

No. 28 on arrival at Ditton Priors, 21st September, 1938. Note the top of the Abdon Quarry Co.'s tar plant behind the station. *N. How Collection*

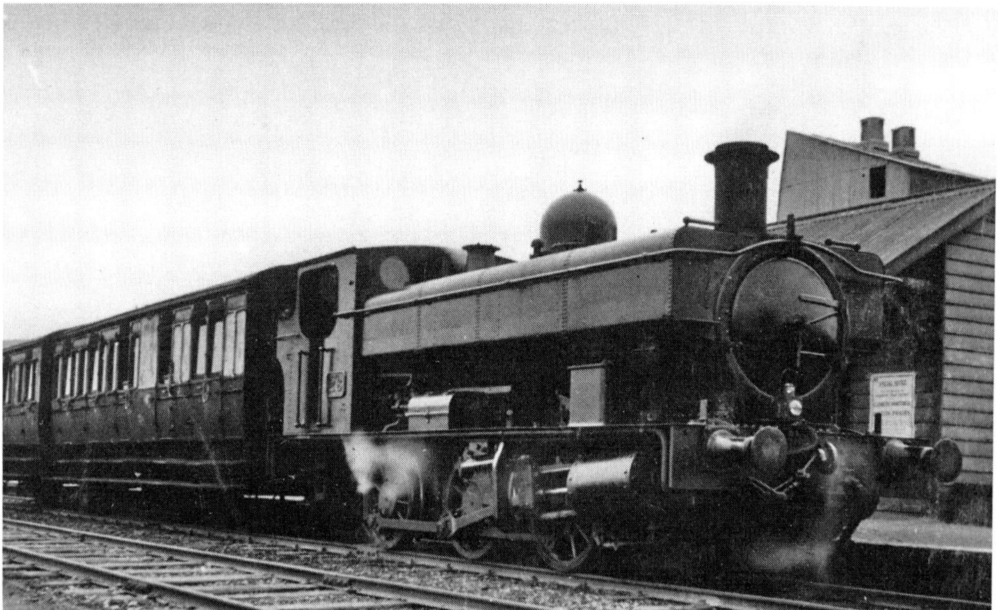

Cleobury Mortimer & Ditton Priors Light Railway.

Taken over by Great Western Ry – June 1922

TIME TABLE

NOVEMBER 2nd, 1921, and until further notice

WEEK DAYS ONLY.—MIXED TRAINS.

TUESDAYS AND THURSDAYS EXCEPTED.

UP.			A (Mons., Weds., & Sats. only)	B (Fridays only)	C (Weds., & Sats. only)
			A.M.	P.M.	P.M.
DITTON PRIORS	...	dep.	11 0	12 30	3 50
Cleobury North Crossing	...	pass	D	D	—
BURWARTON	...	dep.	11 15	12 45	4 0
Aston Botterell Siding	... ...	pass	—	—	—
STOTTESDON	...	dep.	11 30	1 0	4 10
Prescott Siding	... ...	pass	—	—	—
Detton Ford Siding	... ...	,,	D	D	—
Chilton Siding	... ...	,,	—	—	—
CLEOBURY TOWN	...	arr.	12 5	1 29	4 45
,, ,,	...	dep.	12 6	1 30	
CLEOBURY MORTIMER JUNC.		arr.	12 20	1 45	

DOWN.			A (Mons., Weds., & Sats. only)	B (Fridays only)	C (Weds., & Sats. only)
			A.M.	A.M.	P.M.
CLEOBURY MORTIMER JUNC.		dep.	9 18	10 55	2 30
CLEOBURY TOWN	...	arr.	9 28	11 5	2 40
,, ,,	...	dep.	9 30	11 7	2 45
Chilton Siding	... ...	pass	—	—	—
Detton Ford Siding	... ...	,,	D	D	D
Prescott Siding	... ...	,,	D	D	D
STOTTESDON	..	dep.	9 55	11 30	3 5
Aston Botterell Siding	...	pass	D	D	D
BURWARTON	...	dep.	10 13	11 45	3 20
Cleobury North Crossing	...	pass	D	D	D
DITTON PRIORS	...	arr.	10 30	12 0	3 35

A Will run on Mondays, Wednesdays, and Saturdays only. Every exertion will be made for the 11.0 a.m. train from Ditton Priors to connect with the Great Western Company's train due to leave Cleobury Mortimer Junction at 12.38 p.m., but the Company cannot be responsible for any delay caused through late arrival.

B Will run on Fridays only.

C Will run on Wednesdays and Saturdays only.

D Calls if required.

Trains will not run on Christmas Day or Good Friday.

The Company do not guarantee that the trains shall start or arrive at the times printed, and liability cannot be accepted for any delay caused through late running of the trains.

E. J. MORRIS, General Manager

Cleobury Mortimer, October 20th, 1921.

H. G. Perkins, Printer, Load Street, Bewdley.

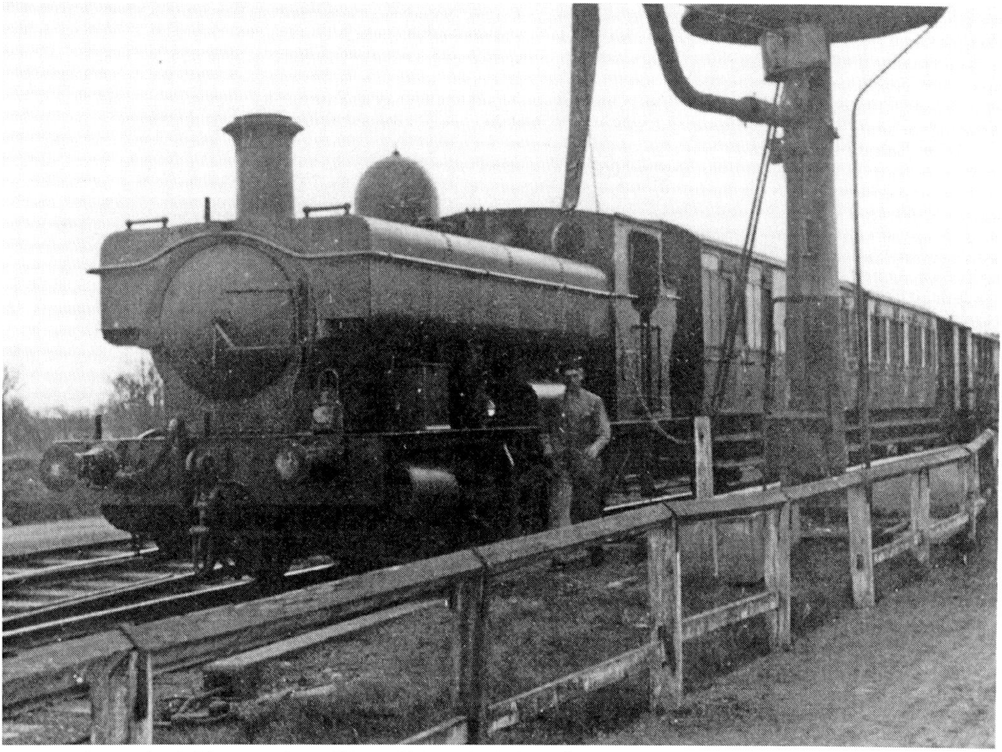

No. 29 on the 3.36 pm train at Ditton Priors, 30th March, 1938. *D.J. Powell/R.S. Carpenter*

Ditton Priors station looking north on 30th March, 1938. *R.K. Cope*

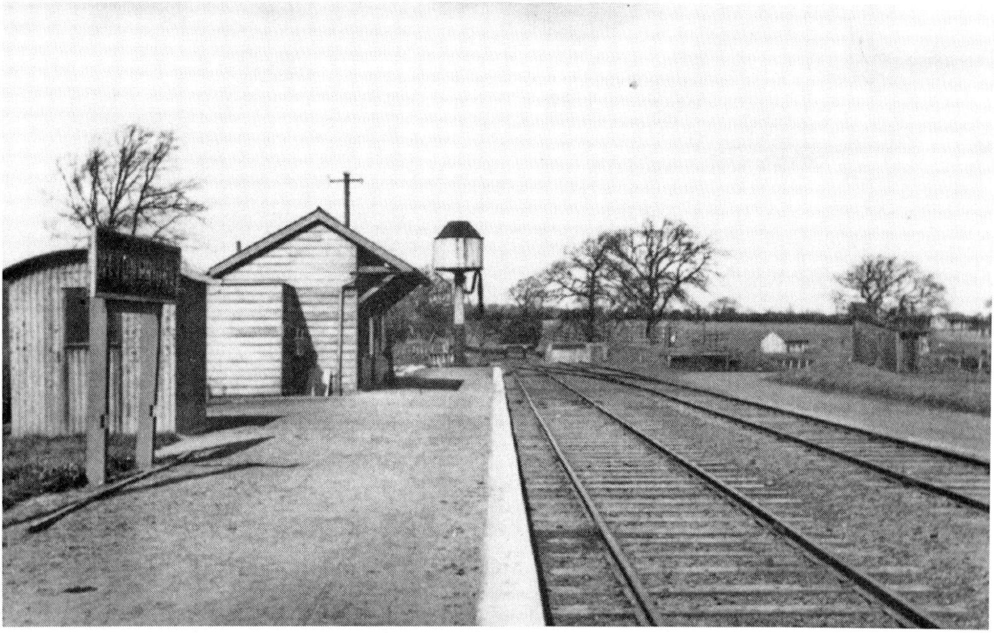

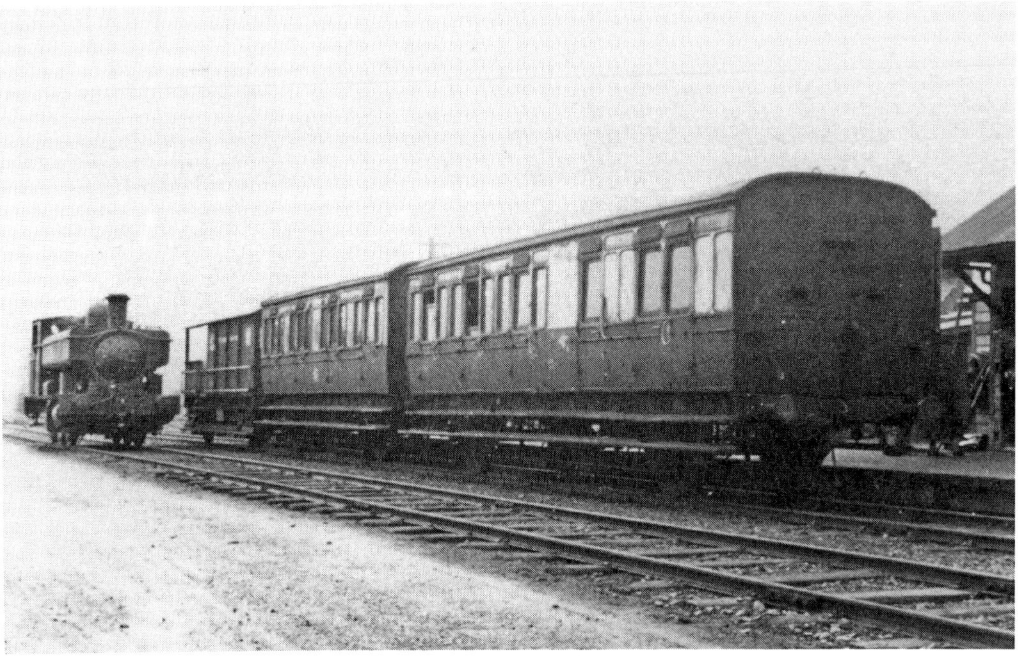

No. 28 running round at Ditton Priors 24th September, 1938. *R.K. Cope*

The end of the line at Ditton Priors station from the buffer stops, 24th April, 1962. Note the RNAD locomotive shed in the distance beyond the wagons on the left. *Author*

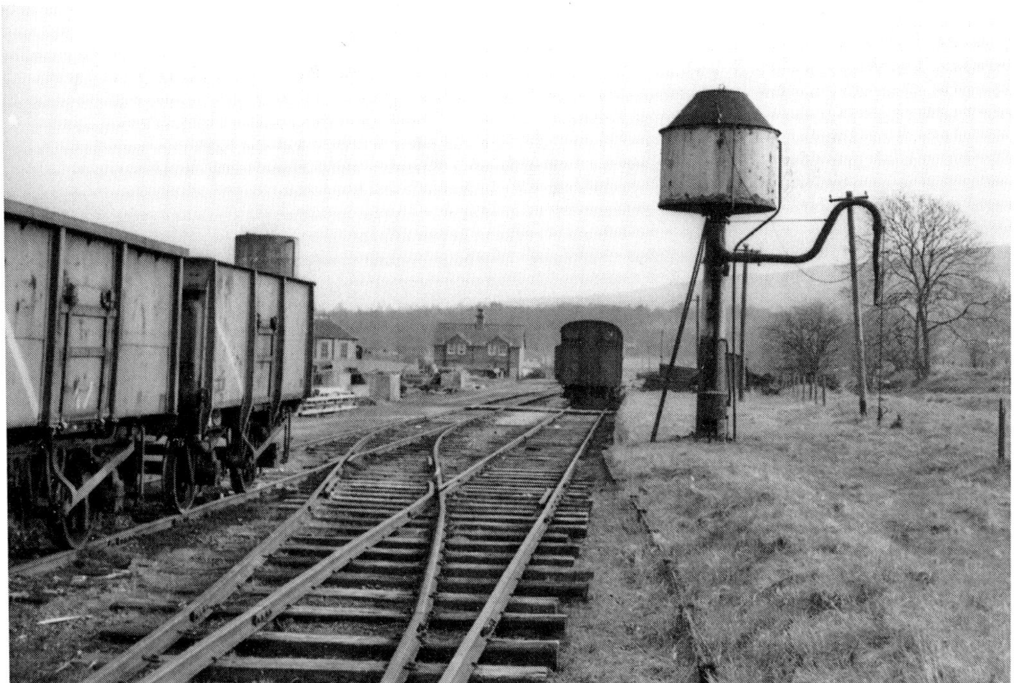

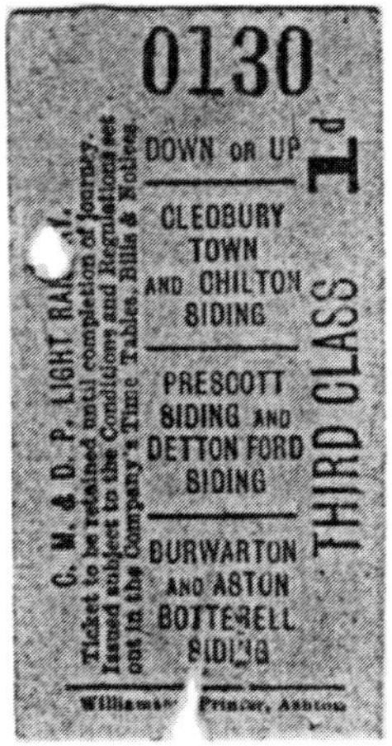

Dark blue

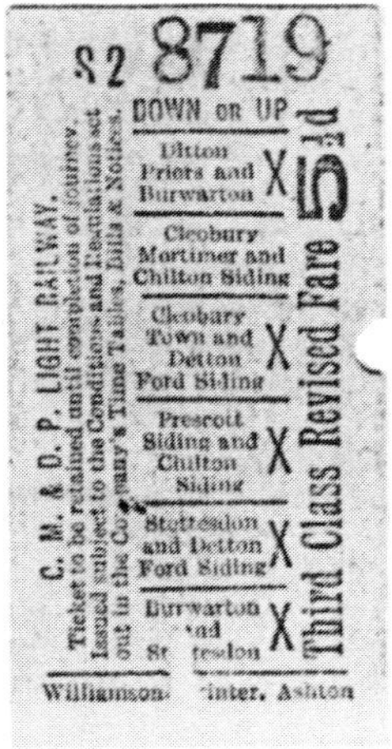

Lilac

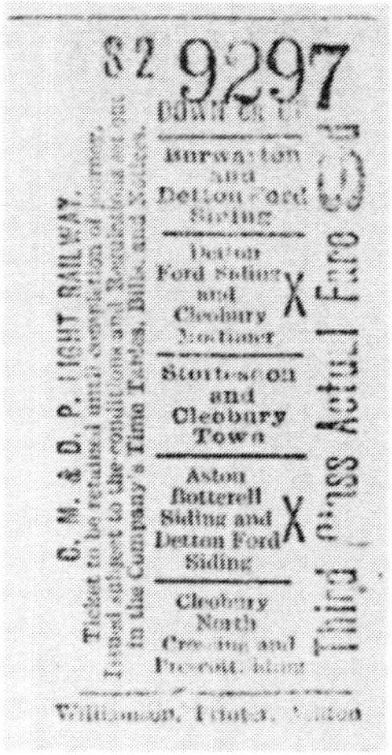

White

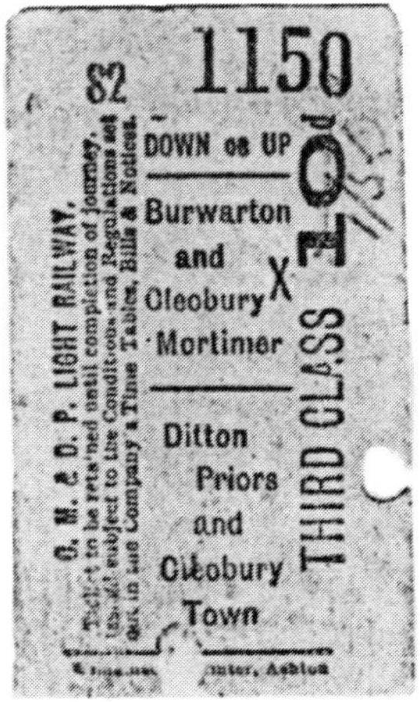

Pale Blue

Below: Rear of 1d. ticket.

Below Right: Rear of 9*d*. ticket. The advetisement for C.S. Corbett & Son also appears on the rear of the 5½*d*. and 10*d*. tickets.

D.G. Geldard

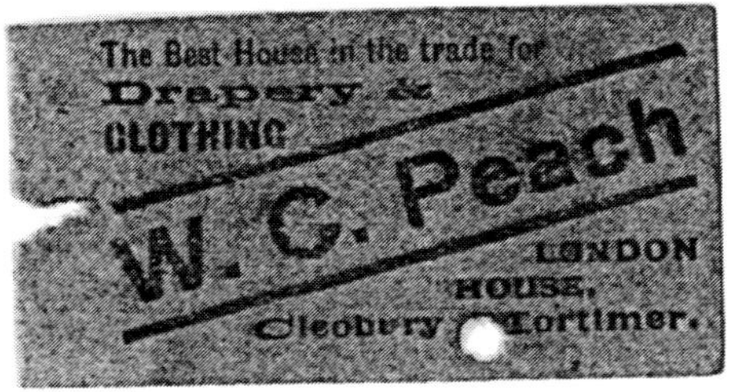

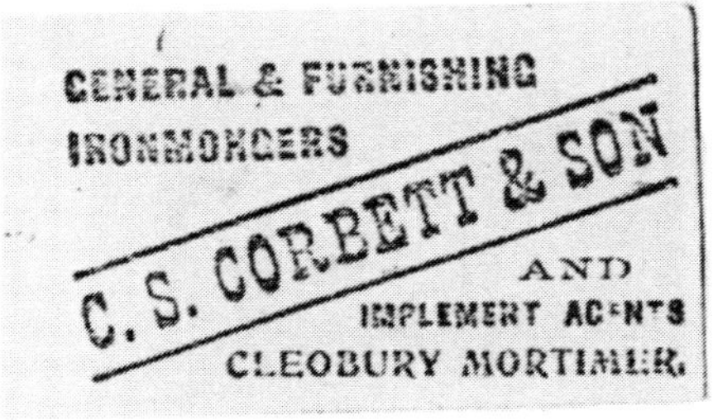

service, but involved the company in the cost of running the train back light.

Tickets, as already mentioned, were issued on the train by the guard. They originally cost 1*d*. a mile single, third class, and 1½*d*. a mile single, first class. The CM&DPLR never issued ordinary return tickets, although it did provide market and privilege returns. It seems that soon after the line opened a minimum 2*d*. fare was established, and fares were rounded up to the nearest whole penny. A journey over the entire length of the line cost 1s. Later revised fares were introduced, ranging from 3½*d*. up to 1*s*. 9*d*. for a single journey between Cleobury Mortimer and Ditton Priors. When the railway was independent they were of the paper Williamson type, but later, under the GWR they were of light card. The CM&DPLR timetable for November, 1921 (*shown on page 45*) shows that the company considered Ditton Priors, Burwarton, Stottesdon, and Cleobury Town to be stations. Apart from Cleobury North Crossing, the other stopping places were mere sidings!

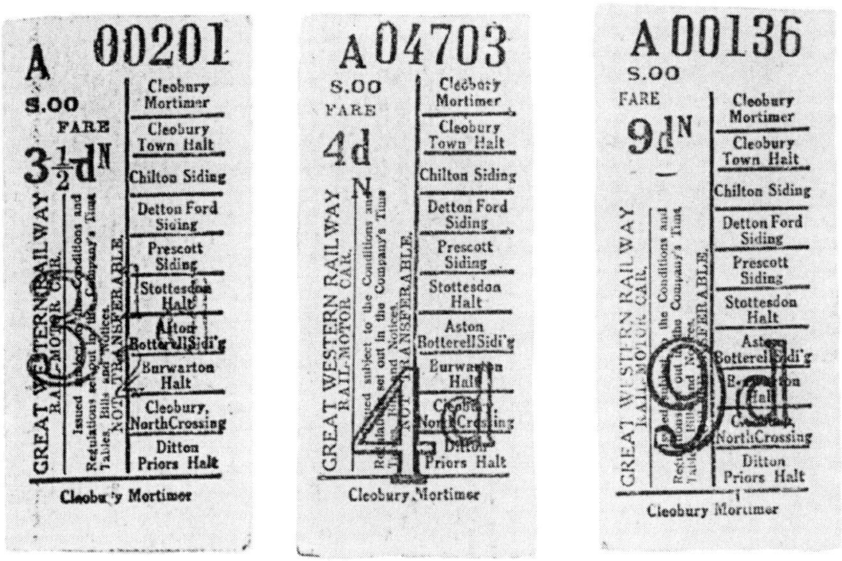

Tickets issued by the GWR. *John Strange*

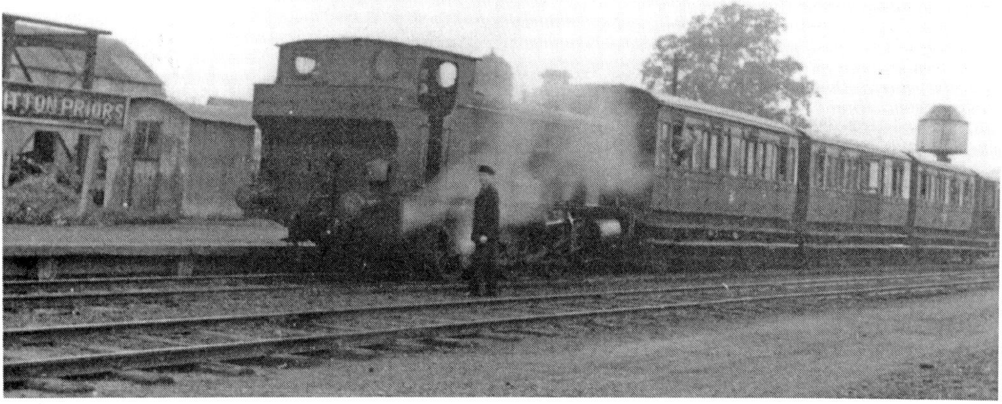

The last passenger train from Ditton Priors prepares to leave, 24th September, 1938.
D.J. Powell

Passengers lean out of the windows of the last passenger train at Cleobury Town Halt, 24th September, 1938.
R.K. Cope

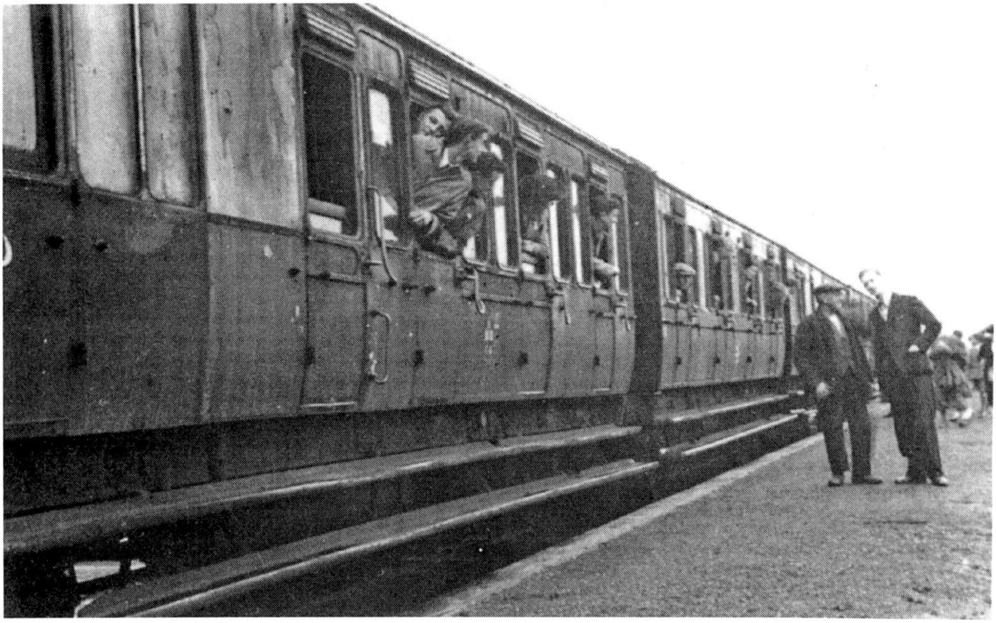

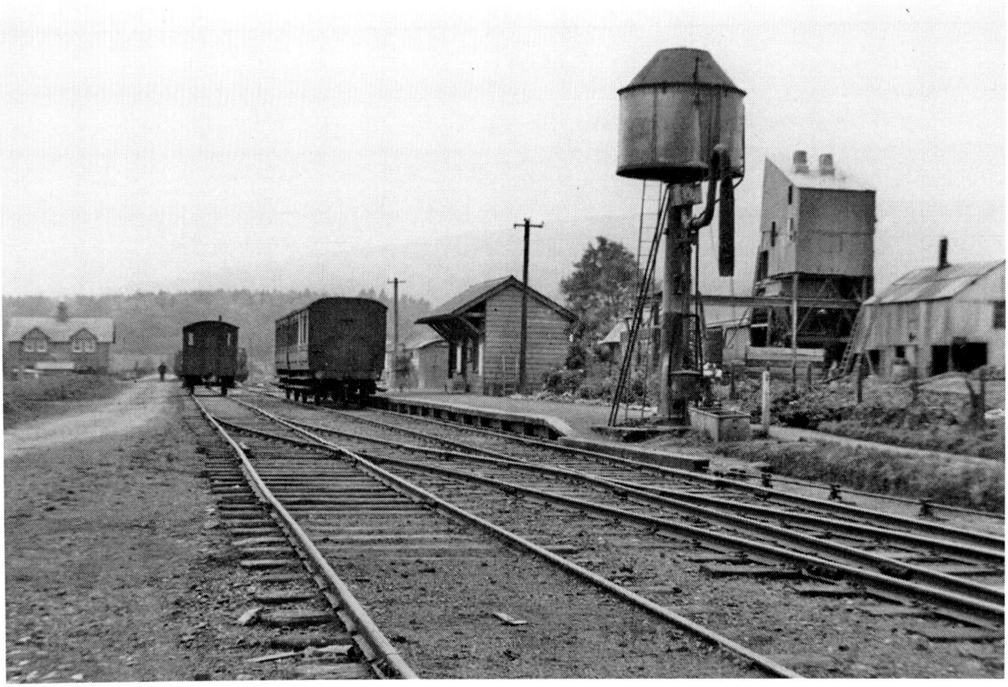

Ditton Priors in 1938; note the tarmac plant to the right. The stone processing plant lay beyond it.
D.J. Powell/LGRP

Kingswood shunting in the Abdon Clee Quarry yard at Ditton Priors. *F. Jones*

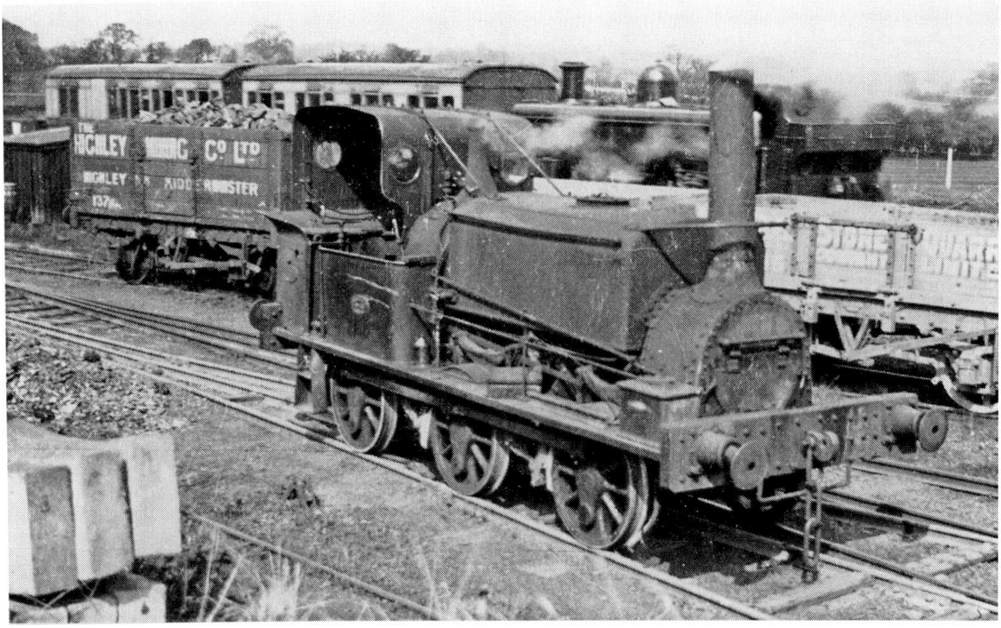

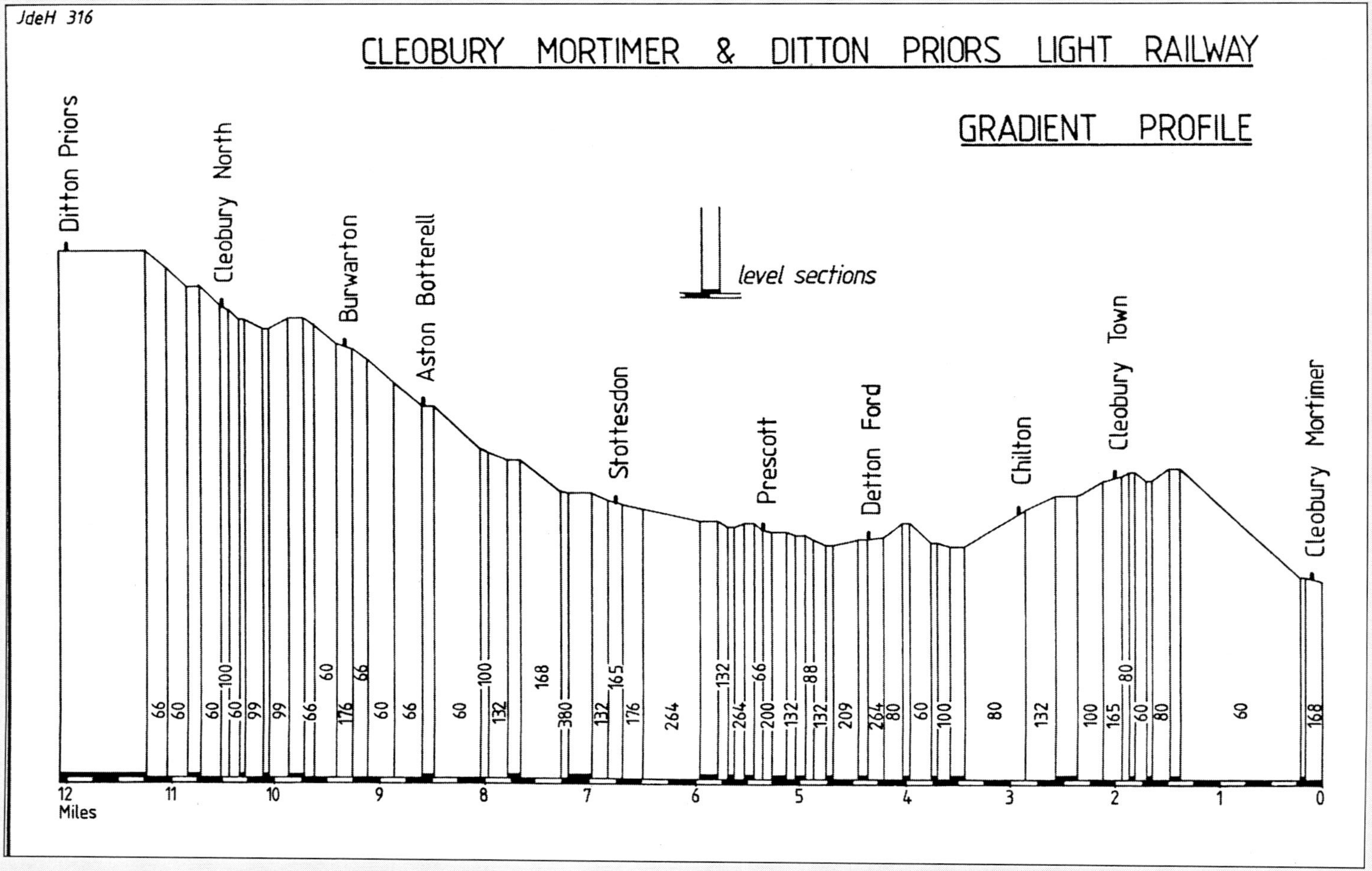
JdeH 316
CLEOBURY MORTIMER & DITTON PRIORS LIGHT RAILWAY
GRADIENT PROFILE
level sections
Ditton Priors
Cleobury North
Burwarton
Aston Botterell
Stottesdon
Prescott
Detton Ford
Chilton
Cleobury Town
Cleobury Mortimer
Miles

Chapter Six

The Abdon Clee Stone Quarries

In view of the very close association of the Abdon Clee quarries with the fortunes of the CM&DPLR, further mention of them must be made. (Those concerned to read a very detailed account of the quarries and their operation would do well to study Chapter 9 of the book on the CM&DP by W. Smith and K.Beddoes.)

In the early years of the quarries much of the stone was used for roadmaking, and for setts to be laid in conjunction with street tramway schemes. In World War I, however, the stone company decided to diversify by setting up a concrete works at Ditton Priors, utilising crushed dhustone and cement. At the time this was a particularly imaginative idea, because it envisaged the manufacture of parts for a prefabricated building system, using a 'post and panel' method. As has been noticed, a number of buildings using this system were constructed on the route of the light railway, but a notable feature of the idea was the fact that the standardised parts could be fitted together readily by unskilled labour. Before long the stone company enjoyed some justifiable success from this venture.

The quarry railway made connection with the CM&DP through sidings at the concrete works behind the passenger platform at Ditton Priors. From the junction it almost immediately began to curve away south-westwards and upwards. After about half a mile the single track passed under a road bridge at Oakwood, and formed a wagon exchange loop at the foot of the huge rope-worked incline that extended right up on to the Abdon Clee. At Oakwood two men were employed to maintain track and equipment, the incline functioning on the self-acting principle whereby loaded wagons descending would haul empty wagons up. The gradient on the lowest part of the incline was not so severe as to prevent adhesion working, and it is understood that on occasions an engine might venture on to it. After a further half mile the route came to two quite closely grouped overbridges where the steepest part of the incline began, rising on a gradient mostly of about 1 in 8, although for one short portion it may have been as much as 1 in 5. The track also divided near these overbridges to form a loop, or 'turnout' as it was here called, to enable ascending and descending wagons to pass one another. Above the turnout the track took the form of three rails, the central rail being common for traffic in both directions.

Approaching the summit of the incline, 1,600 feet above sea level, the gradient eased to 1 in 12 and then 1 in 16 or less. Set back a short distance from the summit, but still in the same straight line followed by the incline, was the brakehouse and drum over which the rope worked. The last quarter mile or so of track then curved sharply away round the hill to the quarry, the crushing plant and the stone storage area. The facilities at the summit included small, but separate, sheds to accommodate both a standard gauge engine used to move wagons to the head of the incline, and narrow gauge motive power used around the quarry itself.

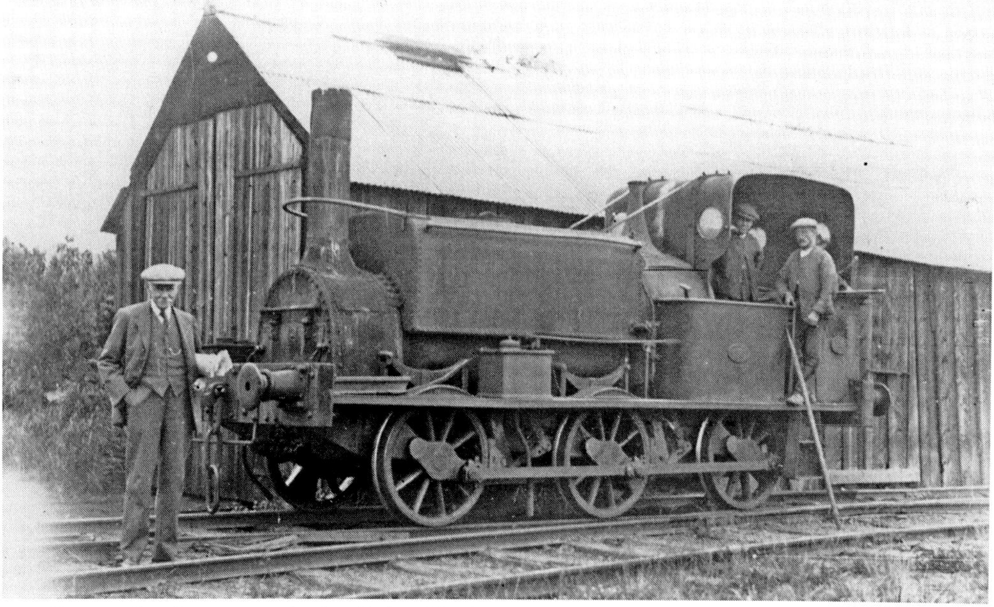

Kingswood and crew outside the Abdon Clee locomotive shed at Ditton Priors.
F. Jones Collection

Fleetwood in the Abdon Clee Quarry yard at Ditton Priors. *F. Jones Collection*

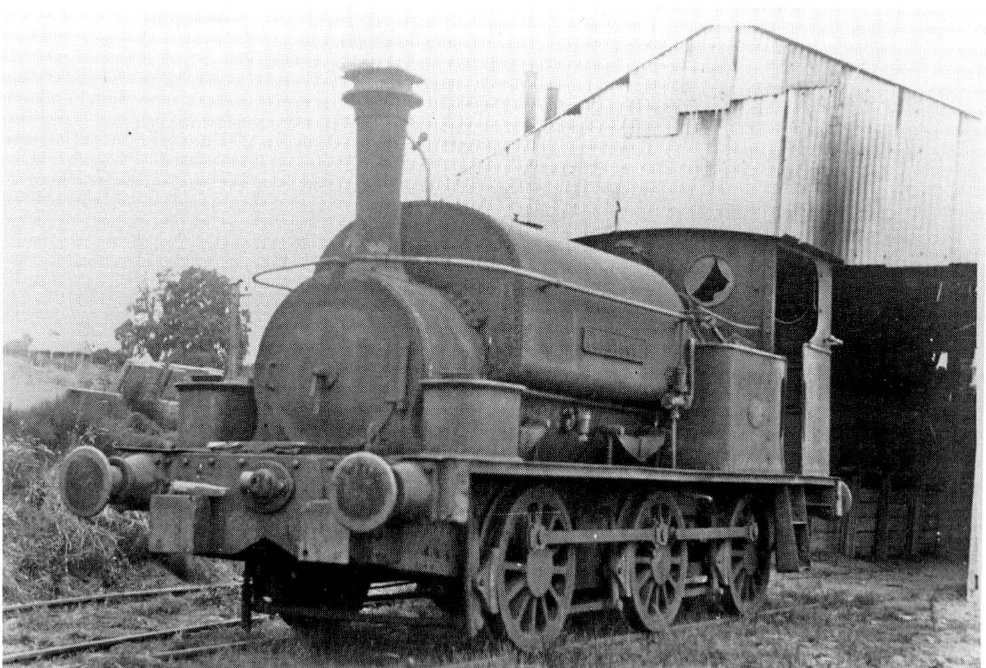

From this short description of the line it will be evident that the Abdon Clee incline followed the usual pattern for self-acting inclines. In consequence it may suffice to be brief in describing its operation. Loaded stone wagons were moved to the top of the incline, and arranged usually in sets of three, the rope being attached to a fourth vehicle called a 'dummy'. Simultaneously, three empty wagons would 'be connected to the other end of the rope ready for the ascent. After a telephone call from the brakesman to Ditton Priors yard, and an exchange of bells between top and bottom to indicate that everything was in order, the loaded wagons would be allowed to run under gravity, hauling the empties up. At the turnout their safe passage was assisted by check rails. Speed was governed by the brakesman controlling the large incline drum, and in spite of a few colourful local tales it is thought that speeds were quite modest, and normally never exceeded 15, or at most 20 mph.

Prior to World War I stone was hauled about within the quarry by horses. At some uncertain date a 2 ft gauge engine was acquired, and reference has been found to a locomotive named *Sedgley* being on the Abdon Clee in 1915. Later, at about the end of the war, two 2 ft gauge four-wheel Simplex petrol locomotives, Nos. 848 and 1029, formerly of the War Department came into employment. The use of a third Simplex has been reported; suffice to say that locally they became known as 'Whizz-bangs' - apparently from a propensity to backfire.

Some four standard gauge engines were used by the Abdon Clee company. The first was *Fleetwood*, previously mentioned in connection with the opening of the CM&DPLR. This was by Hudswell, Clarke & Co., No. 313 of 1888, an 0-6-0ST with 13 in. x 20 in. cylinders, and 3 ft 3 in. diameter driving wheels. It originated with Thomas Riley, a contractor of Fleetwood, and came to the quarry via Messrs Bott & Stennett and the T.A. Walker, Manchester Ship Canal contract. Two other engines were *Trent* and *Kingswood*, both inside cylinder 0-6-0ST's obtained through Bott & Stennett and built by Manning, Wardle & Co., being Nos. 626 of 1876 and 729 of 1880 respectively. The fourth engine was not acquired until 1934, following a breakdown with *Fleetwood.* This was an 0-6-0 side tank with outside cylinders, built in 1917 by Kerr, Stuart & Co. of Stoke-on-Trent, and very similar to two side tank locomotives supplied at the same period to the North Staffordshire Railway. This engine, *Park,* came to Ditton Priors from T.W. Ward (Grays Department) in 1934, but as activity at the quarry was already in decline it was sold on to R.R. Paton Ltd, of Cardiff by November, 1937. In June 1938, it went to South Wales Coalite Ltd, Wern Tarw colliery, and after World War II it was in use at NCB Newlands, near Margam. The livery of *Park,* like that of *Trent,* was green, but whereas *Park* (like *Fleetwood,* worked between Ditton Priors and the foot of the incline, *Trent* spent most of its time working at the summit. *Kingswood* appears to have had spells both above and below the incline, and like *Fleetwood* carried a maroon livery.

The early history of the quarry has been mentioned, but in operation it got off to an unfortunate start. On almost the very first trip the rope broke and the loaded wagons hurtled down the incline, derailed and smashed themselves to splinters near the top of the turnout. Fortunately there were no casualties, but the proprietors took care that the next rope installed could take the strain.

However, after a period of satisfactory use, the second rope became so worn that one morning in the 1930s it also parted. On this occasion the wagons were on the turnout, in the steepest part of the incline. One set crashed at the bottom of the turnout but the others carried on down the line under their own momentum. By the time they got to the end of the slope they were going a good speed, and, in the words of one local, 'they shot halfway through Ditton Priors!' How this is to be interpreted is a matter of personal choice - what does seem certain is that it caused quite a stir in the community, although no damage (other than to the railway equipment) was done on either occasion. Although there was at least one fatality on the Abdon Clee incline in addition to the death of Driver Revell on the incline in 1908, the Abdon Clee stone quarries witnessed very few serious accidents.

From the start the stone traffic was prosperous - 117,769 tons in 1913, compared with the estimated 100,000 tons (although the first figure does include that obtained from Detton Ford). When at its zenith, on the Abdon Clee, some 14 or 15 trips a day were necessary on the incline, but after World War I the traffic began to dwindle, and continued to do so right through the 'twenties'. By 1928 the Clee Hill Granite Co. connected with Detton Ford was worked out and two or three years later the Abdon Clee Company began to open up a part of the dhustone deposit not easily accessible for the railway. Thus all traffic fell off quite quickly, ceasing completely in 1936. Equipment was left where it was, however, for some time, and Ditton Priors yard became the home of *Fleetwood* lying derelict until it was eventually cut up on the spot.

One cause of the failure of the stone traffic was that with the development of modern tarred roadmaking methods the dhustone came less and less into demand. In actual fact the dhustone was a type of granite, and generally such dolerites are, when fresh, of great economic value, being then particularly hard heavy and tough. However, in the Clee Hills the geology was such that the hard alkaline dolerite only formed a cap to the hills, lower layers being of carboniferous rock and old red sandstone.

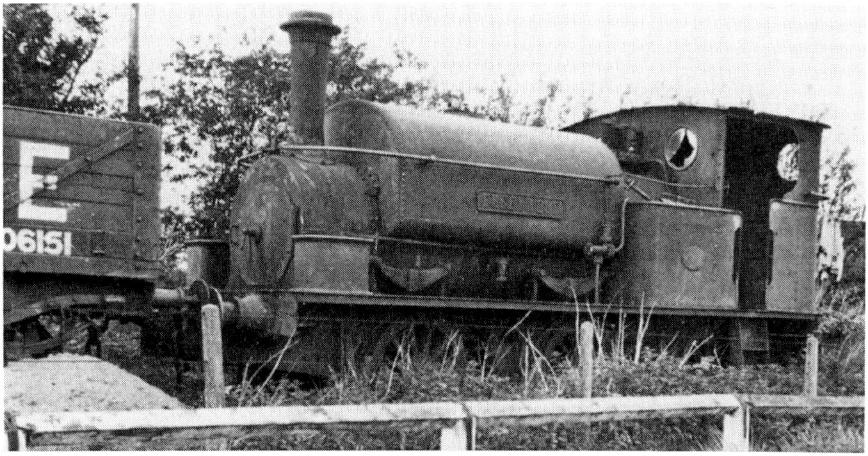

Fleetwood in the Abdon Clee sidings at Ditton Priors. *Lens of Sutton*

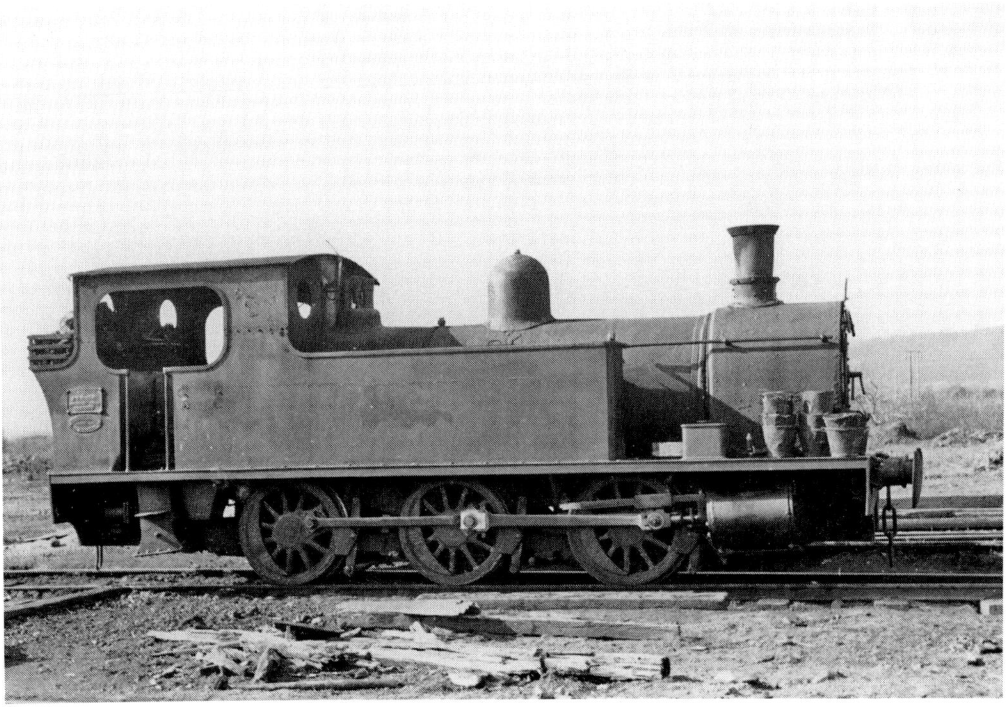

Former Abdon Clee locomotive *Park* at NCB Newlands, South Wales. *F. Jones*

A view looking up the Abdon Clee incline 6th August, 1932. *D.J. Powell*

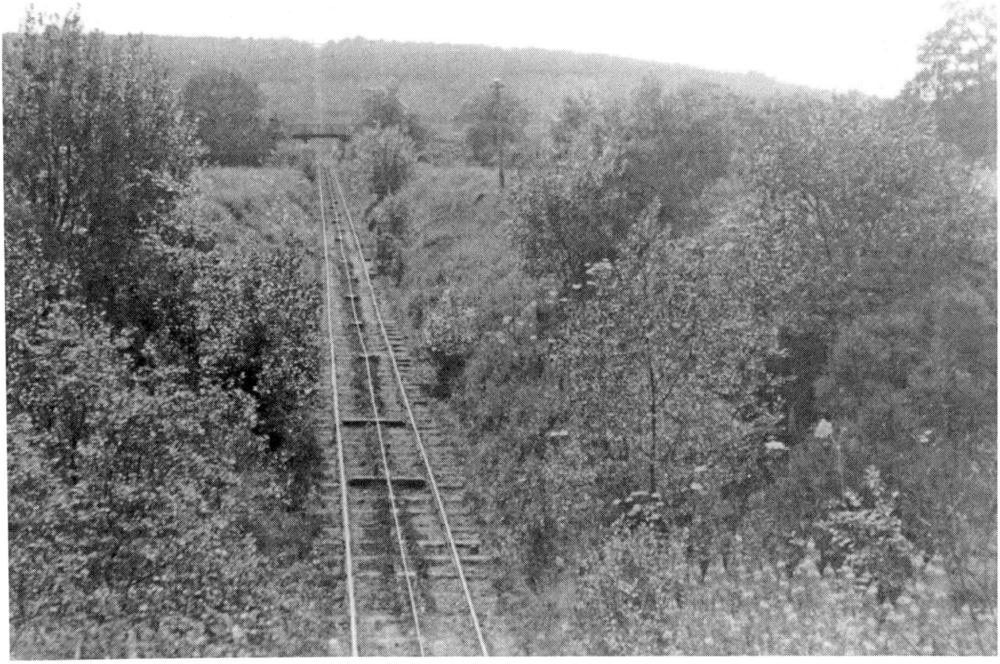

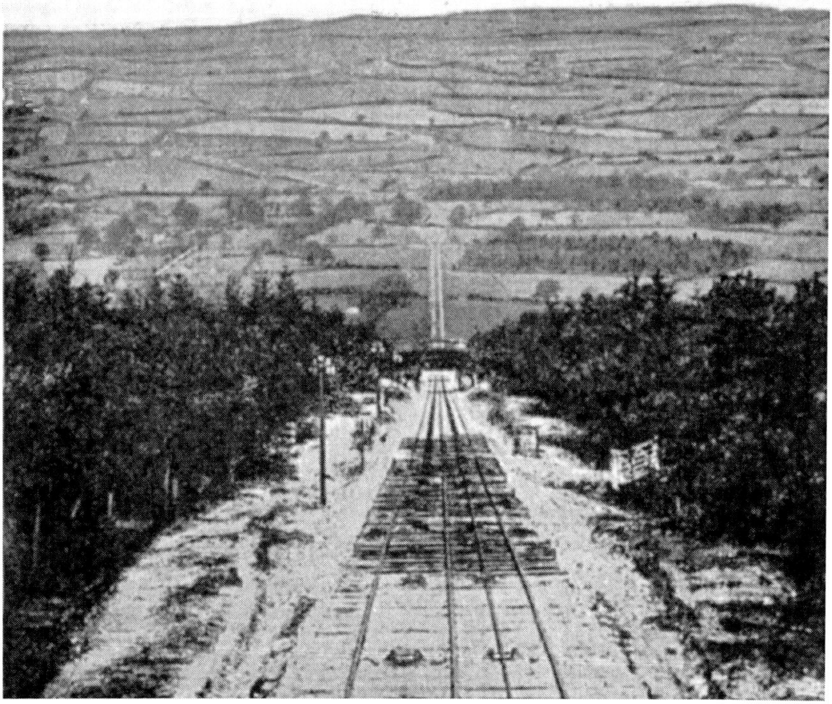

A view looking down the Abdon Clee incline. *R.W. Kidner Collection*

Actually not the entrance to a jungle, but the view from beneath the overbridge at the bottom of the Abdon Clee Incline'turnout', towards the summit, taken in September 1962. Part of the road built on the track-bed may be seen in the distance. *M.R.C. Price*

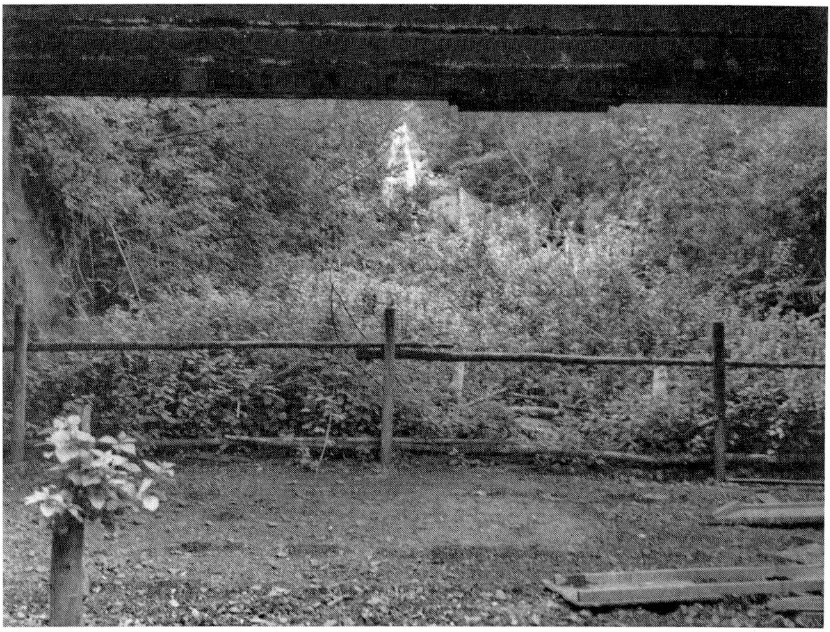

Chapter Seven

The Great Western and the Admiralty

Under the Railway Act of 1921, the Cleobury Mortimer and Ditton Priors Light Railway was absorbed into the Great Western Railway on and from 1st January, 1922. The line was slow to change; some equipment came in for alteration or replacement (notably, of course, the rolling stock), but on the whole it kept itself to itself. The loss of independence and, inevitably, of complete local control seemed to induce a certain drowsiness unknown before. This was accentuated by the gradual falling off of the stone traffic.

An increasing threat over the years was, needless to say, the internal combustion engine. The Shropshire hills gradually lost their old fears for motorists, and use of the railway by farmers in particular, became less. Former features, like regular livestock traffic to Kidderminster on market days, almost completely ceased. Furthermore, the passenger traffic in such a sparsely populated area had never been great, and now it dwindled; the old optimistic ideals about holiday and tourist developments were never really realised. Cleobury Mortimer was not without its character and history, and its excellent situation relative to the Clee Hills had once made it a potential inland resort, but the commercial exploitation of the Clees on the one hand and the growth in popularity of the Malverns, 20 miles to the south on the other, between them removed any serious possibility of development.

The Great Western did not stress the importance of the CM&DP either; throughout the period of its jurisdiction not a single station (not even Ditton Priors) was allowed any title more noble than 'halt'. Hence it came as no surprise when the GWR announced that the passenger services were to be withdrawn. But some years before this actually happened two interesting events took place, then a source of speculation and consternation (to the light railway staff at least) and even now an interesting subject for discussion. It seems that the Great Western had to resort to new traction in the absence of No. 28 at Swindon and so, in 1931, it dispatched 0-6-0 outside cylinder side tank No. 2197 to the railway for trials. It had been built in 1909 as No. 8, *Pioneer*, of the old Burry Port and Gwendraeth Valley Railway. It was not a success, and was sent back to South Wales, to survive until 1952. Earlier in 1931 the bulky form of 0-6-0 inside cylinder side tank No. 803, formerly *Ravelston* of the Llanelly and Mynydd Mawr Railway, had appeared on the scene. This proved to be too heavy and was returned whence it came (via a brief spell of shunting at Worcester) to live on until 1951.

The official announcement of passenger closure came in July 1938; trains to be cancelled were the 9.30 am, 2.24 pm (Wednesdays only) and 5.20 pm from Cleobury Mortimer to Ditton Priors, and in the reverse direction from Ditton Priors those at 11.10 am, 3.50 pm (Wednesdays only) and 6.23 pm. This was to take effect on and from Monday 26th September, 1938, the last passenger trains actually running on 24th September, as there was, and never had been, a Sunday service. This actual event was, from all accounts, rather surprisingly

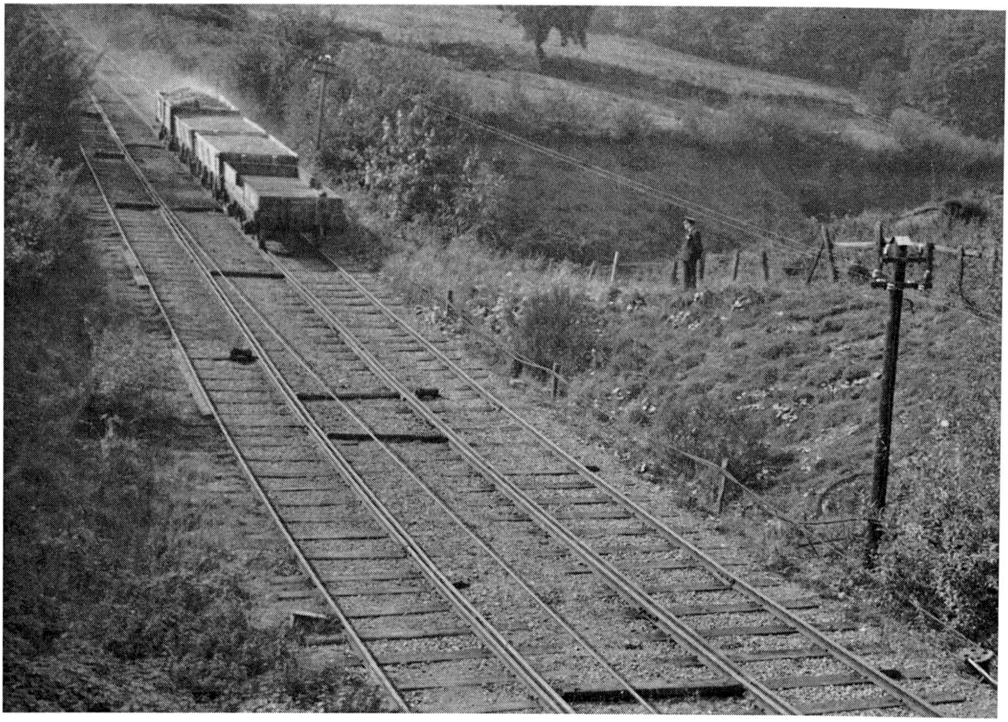

A run of stone wagons on the incline, 1933. *Weh-Lyn Records*

A postcard view of the stone quarry works on Abdon Clee. The locomotive is *Trent.* *D.J. Powell*

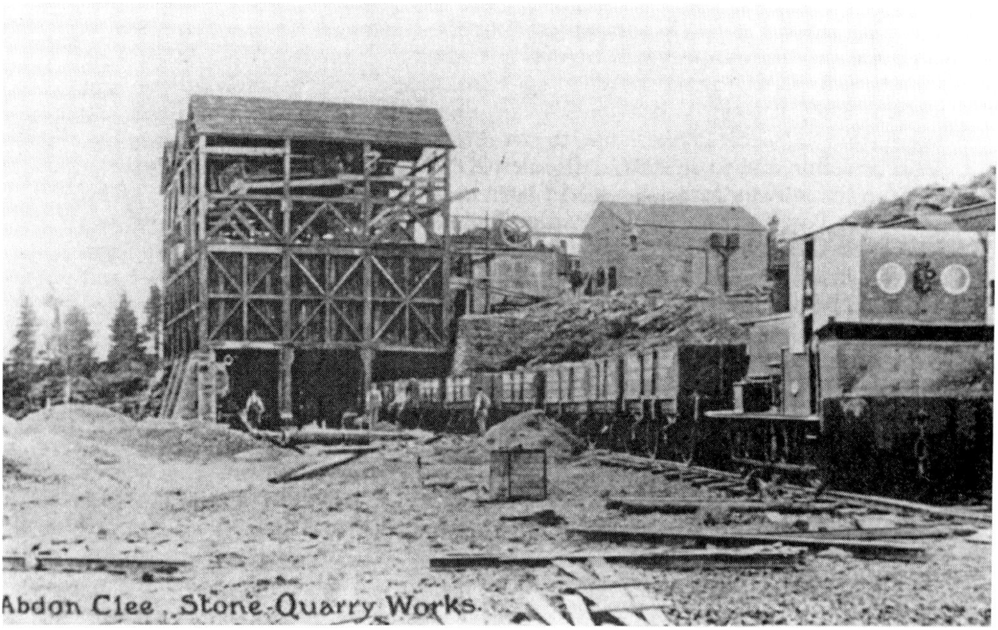

accompanied by the sort of branch closing-day scenes that have been much more familiar since the war than before. Indeed, the *Railway Magazine*, subsequently, published some entertaining and informative notes of the affair.

On Saturday, September 24th, Cleobury Mortimer station, on the GWR line from Bewdley to Wooferton, was invaded by a crowd of railway enthusiasts from various parts of the country who had come to travel by the last passenger train on the Ditton Priors Light Railway. This invasion apparently took the Great Western Railway by surprise; the branch train, which contrary to customary practice was not mixed, consisted of 0-6-0PT, No. 28, and two four-wheel gas-lit carriages, dingy but comparatively comfortable. When, however, another train arrived from Kidderminster and disgorged yet more enthusiasts determined to be present at the obsequies, it became evident that this accommodation would not be sufficient, and two other carriages of the same type, but in a more dilapidated condition, were requisitioned from a siding and added to the train. Undeterred by a dull and misty afternoon, those of the party who owned cameras surrounded 'the outfit' (as someone described it), and opened fire from all angles. The station staff turned a conveniently blind eye on minor breaches of the regulations and one enterprising gentleman, profiting thereby, climbed up on to the platform of a bracket signal and took a bird's eye view of the scene. The booking clerk was meanwhile running to and fro issuing excess fare tickets to all who had come from stations beyond Cleobury Mortimer, as there were no through bookings from outside to places on the branch.

When the furious energy of the photographers had been somewhat expended and everybody was aboard, including a few local people who were going home by this way for the last time we moved out at 5.45 pm 25 minutes behind schedule, but who was worrying? Stops were made at all 'sidings', and 'halts' on the way to Ditton Priors . . . and at about every stopping place there was a little gathering of folk, some of whom had come in cars, to cheer and wave us as we left. Slowing to the prescribed 10 mph and whistling prodigiously before we reached each of the numerous level crossings . . . we eventually arrived at Ditton Priors Halt at 6.47 pm after a journey which, though most interesting, could hardly have been called smooth. Officially, we were due to arrive at 6.11, and should have left again for Cleobury Mortimer at 6.23. But the entire trainload turned out at Ditton Priors in order to make a tour of inspection and indulge in further photography. Souvenirs of the occasion were created on the spot by placing coins on the rails of the loop, to be passed over and flattened by the engine as it ran round the train. One or two persons removed posters giving notice of the withdrawal of the passenger service, and appropriated them.

After No. 28 had taken in water we started off at 6.58 pm bunker first (the locomotive usually faced north towards the terminus) for the final run. A long shrill blast announced our departure, but there was scarcely anyone to see us go by; by this time it was beginning to grow dusk, and there were fewer shouted 'goodbyes' at the halts. We saved a little time on our belated journey, as we were not booked to stop at two of these halts. Once more our recitatives on the whistle proclaimed to the countryside that the last passenger train from Ditton Priors was passing on its way, and would not return. Presently, sitting in almost complete darkness, for the gas-tanks of the carriages were empty, we drew into the station at Cleobury Mortimer with treble and alto whistles blowing, answered by those of the connection to Kidderminster which had been held for nearly a quarter-of-an-hour on our behalf, and with joyous noises from our own party, while a small box of fireworks, handed to the porters before the commencement of the outward trip, was being let off on the platform with fine effect. We were hurried into what should have been the 7.34 pm from Cleobury Mortimer, but which was in fact somewhere about 7.50, and as the train pulled out we looked back and saw our four aged carriages standing in the bay, empty, dark and forlorn, vanishing into the night amid a drifting cloud of steam.

So much for the last day, it was probably the liveliest in the line's history. The fortunes of the railway were now at a nadir. A daily goods in each direction still operated to convey parcels, minerals, livestock and general merchandise to and from all stopping places, except Chilton Siding which, even before the passenger shut-down, had apparently been stripped of all identity. But the future seemed very uncertain until, in 1939, the course of international events saved the situation at its eleventh hour.

The Admiralty arrived to take over a tract of country, over a mile long, in the Little Leasowes area immediately east of the CM&DPLR between Cleobury North Crossing and Ditton Priors and here the many buildings of the Royal Naval Armament Depot, Ditton Priors, were erected. Thereafter the daily goods worked through the war as a supply train, serving not only the new depot but also those dumps established early in hostilities at the stations on the railway. The amount of shunting involved could leave locomotives very short of water, and it is said that on occasions RNAD staff had to arrange for a fire tender to meet engines at a level crossing in order to replenish its tanks. At the end of the war, a new exchange siding and water column was provided at Kennel crossing, just above Cleobury North. Ironically, by 1946 the requirements of the depot had reduced to such an extent that it was only necessary to provide a thrice-weekly service.

Nationalisation had little effect upon the operations of the line. For British Railways, like the Great Western before them, continued to run the supply trains up as far as Cleobury North Crossing. At this point the loaded wagons were passed to the RNAD locomotives in exchange for the empties. The working of the trains right through was terminated for security reasons, although it has been suggested that No. 29 obtained a spark arrester originally, not only to guard against forest fires - an unlikely event in such relatively open country - but to enable it to work safely into the depot itself, if need be. But by the end of the 'forties the CM&DP locomotives only occasionally appeared on the light railway, their place being taken by other pannier tanks from Kidderminster. Several members of the old '2021' class were used at different dates, and at least four - 2034, 2051, 2101 and 2144 carried 'balloon stack' spark arresters for this purpose. In May 1955, the line briefly relived some of its past with the visit of a railfan's excursion. Organised under the auspices of the Stephenson Locomotive Society the train, headed by 'balloon stacked' 0-6-0 pannier tank No. 2144, travelled as far as Cleobury North Crossing only.

The RNAD locomotives have all been diesel. It is believed that an 0-4-0 Planet locomotive worked there for a time, but apart from that they are understood to have been of Ruston and Hornsby design. Three locomotives each weighing 28 tons and having 165 hp engines were supplied to Ditton Priors depot in June 1952, March 1953 and May 1955, the first two having the respective builders serial Nos. 313390 and 319286. An important factor was that they were built to conform with the requirements of the Ministry of Mines, as regards flameproofing.

It was also arranged to supply a petrol driven compressor set for installation in the locomotive shed at Ditton Priors, away from the flame proof area. This would charge the air receiver fitted in the locomotives for starting purposes. Of the three, No. 319286 was apparently transferred away to an Admiralty Depot elsewhere; certainly only two were present in 1965 and these carried the Ditton Priors Yard Nos. 734 and 35. The only item of Admiralty-owned rolling stock on the line was a 20 ton brake van obtained from British Railways.

The RNAD, Ditton Priors, for all its extensive area, was one of the smallest in the United Kingdom, but it survived some immediate post-war cuts in defence establishments. For a while there was actually some increase in activity after depots elsewhere closed. Under the British Transport Commission No. 2 Bill of 1955, the Admiralty became owners of the whole route from Cleobury Mortimer on 1st May, 1957, and operated it entirely from 30th September, 1957, with their own equipment. Thereafter there were two complete train crews, each having an engine driver and two brakesmen/shunters. In addition there were two gangs, each of about six to eight men, to maintain the railway, one being responsible for that length of line up to Stottesdon and the other gang for the remainder. The train service once again became daily and when the RNAD was really busy, two might be run. Even so, the economics of the operation were questionable, and it caused no great surprise when it was announced that the RNAD would close in 1965. It was also obvious that when it shut, the railway would follow it into history.

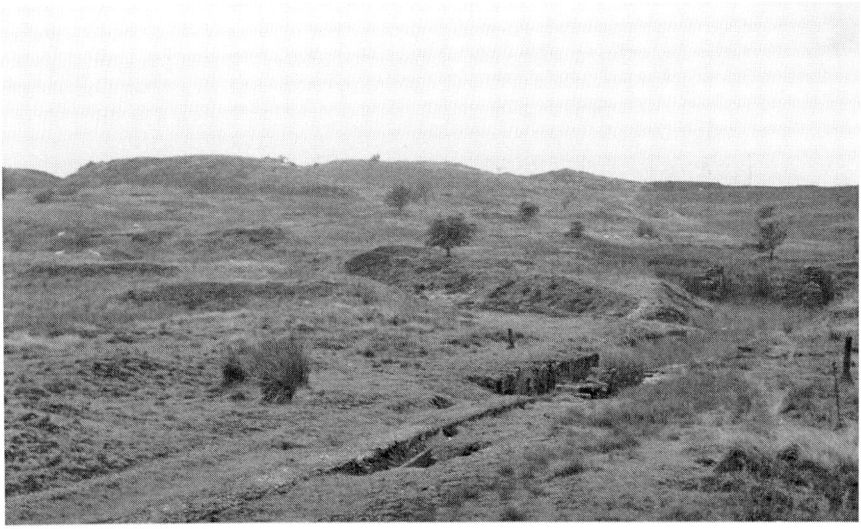

Site of Abdon Clee incline winding house, 1962. Note the bed of the Abdon Clee line curving away to the left towards the stone quarry works. *Author*

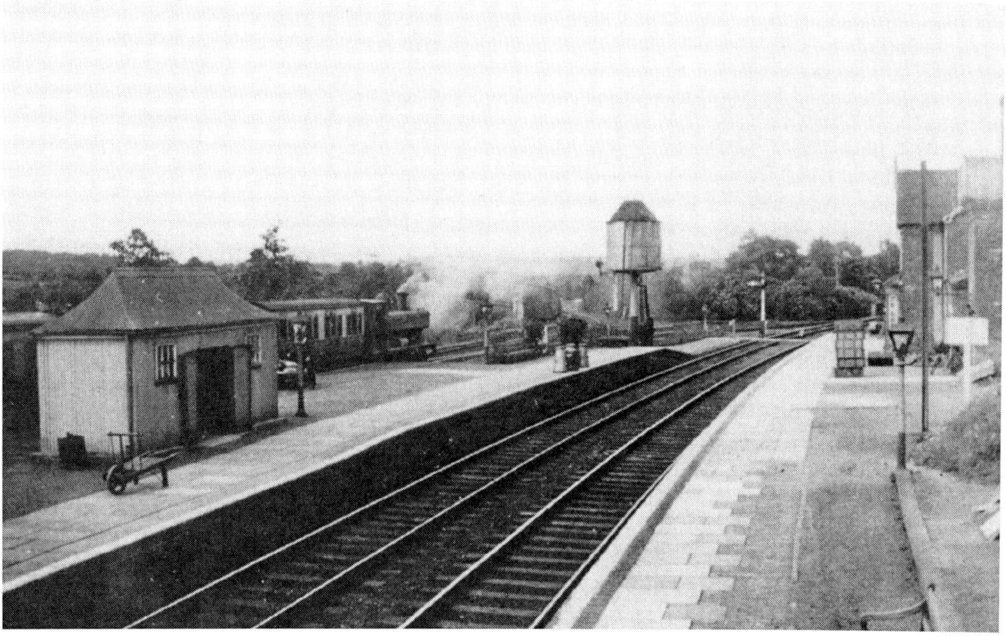

Cleobury Mortimer Junction, showing the Ditton Priors train, 1930. *Mowat Collection*

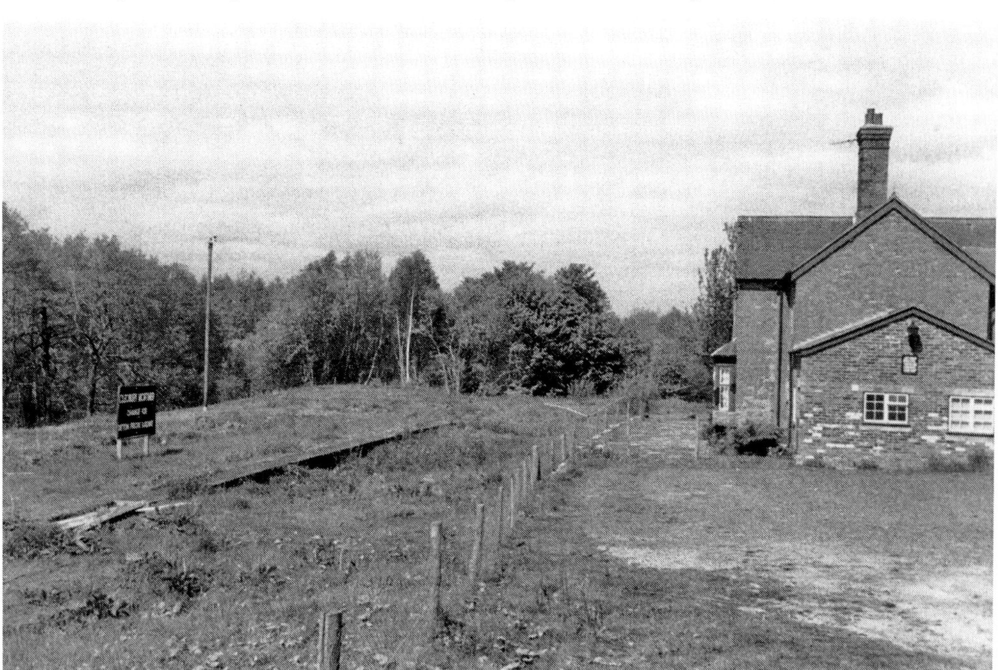

Cleobury Mortimer Junction station site, showing the Ditton Priors platform, 1992. *Author*

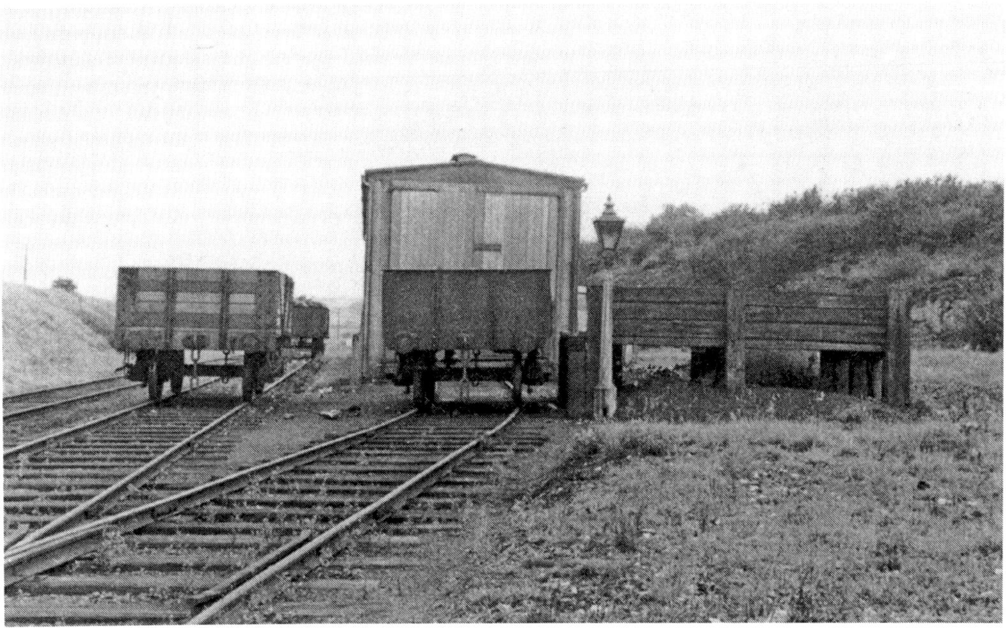

Cleobury Town shed on 24th September, 1938. *D.J. Powell/R.S. Carpenter*

Cleobury Town shed, May 1992. The shed has since been demolished, and much of the site has been redeveloped as a small business park. *Author*

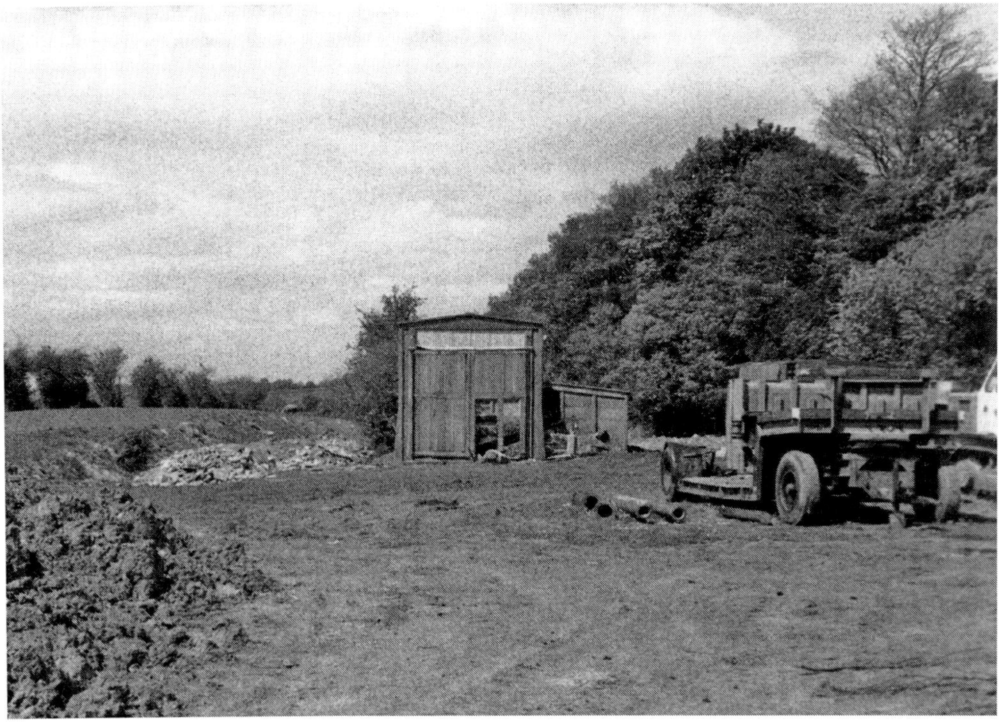

GWR

SPECIAL NOTICE

DISCONTINUANCE OF

PASSENGER TRAIN SERVICE

BETWEEN

CLEOBURY MORTIMER

AND

DITTON PRIORS

The Great Western Railway give notice that on and from MONDAY, SEPTEMBER 26th, 1938, the Passenger Train service on the above Line will be withdrawn and the following trains cancelled :—

9.30 a.m. Cleobury Mortimer to Ditton Priors.
2.24 p.m. (Wednesdays only) Cleobury Mortimer to Ditton Priors.
5.20 p.m. Cleobury Mortimer to Ditton Priors.
11.10 a.m. Ditton Priors to Cleobury Mortimer.
3.50 p.m. (Wednesdays only) Ditton Priors to Cleobury Mortimer.
6.23 p.m. Ditton Priors to Cleobury Mortimer.

The Platforms at the undermentioned places will be closed to Passengers :—

CLEOBURY TOWN HALT
DETTON FORD SIDING
PRESCOTT SIDING
STOTTESDON HALT
ASTON BOTTERELL SIDING
BURWARTON HALT
CLEOBURY NORTH CROSSING
DITTON PRIORS HALT

The Company will continue to run one Goods train in each direction over the Line on week-days only, and so afford facilities for the conveyance of Parcels traffic, Minerals, Livestock and General Merchandise to and from the above-mentioned places.

Particulars of the arrangements may be obtained on application to the Station Master, Cleobury Mortimer, Mr. J. E. Potter, Divisional Superintendent, Worcester (Shrub Hill Station) (Telephone 1530), or Mr. J. A. Warren-King, District Goods Manager, Worcester (Shrub Hill Station) (Telephone 1530).

Paddington Station,
July, 1938.

JAMES MILNE,
General Manager.

P.400. Printed in Great Britain by WYMAN & SONS LTD., London, Reading and Fakenham.—519.

Chapter Eight

Postscript, 1992

The final paragraphs of the first edition were entitled 'Along the Line Today', a heading hardly appropriate thirty years later. Indeed, then it was very much a time of change, and the closure of the CM&DPLR anticipated for 1965 was soon to take place. The Beeching era on British Railways was at its height, and the decline of local railways was rapid. The Tenbury and Bewdley line was closed to passengers from 31st July, 1962, an experimental service of only one passenger train a day each way for the final year having proved to be (not surprisingly) quite unremunerative. A freight service to Tenbury continued for some months, enabling the place to achieve brief notoriety by the publication in the *Daily Telegraph* (30th August, 1962) of an illustrated article describing Tenbury Wells as 'A 12-staff station with no passengers and only one goods train a day'. Such a situation could not last long, and freight facilities were officially withdrawn from 6th January, 1964, after which date goods trains ran as required as far as Cleobury Mortimer for the RNAD, Ditton Priors, traffic only.

The CM&DPLR closed quietly at Easter 1965. According to British Railways, the line closed on and from 16th April 1965, but even a few days later the RNAD authorities were not able to confirm this date. However, it is believed that the last trip was run on 16th April, and certainly when the writer visited Cleobury Town and Ditton Priors a week later, the tracks did not appear to have been used for several days. Not long after, the two diesel locomotives were transferred to other Ministry of Defence establishments, but the railway itself lay dormant for over a year. Eventually the Ministry of Defence advertised the track and other materials for sale by tender, the closing date being 4th October, 1966. The approximate quantities stated included 1,800 tons of rails, 25,000 sleepers and 240 telegraph poles. The demolition contract was awarded to George Cohen, Sons & Co. Ltd, of London, and work began late in the same year, being completed in mid-1967. The RNAD, Ditton Priors, was used for storage for about two years after its closure, the premises being largely in the hands of the American services. Whilst the demolition of the railway was in progress, the contractors had a difference of opinion with the American authorities over the use of oxyacetylene equipment near the depot. Ultimately Cohens' wishes prevailed, but then a sudden decision was taken for the Americans to leave Ditton Priors, and they were out of the depot within three or four days.

By the time Cohens began work, the CM&DPLR was entirely isolated from the national rail network - a curious feature noted on at least one printing of 1 in. Ordnance Survey maps. The railway from Bewdley to Cleobury was dismantled under contract in the latter part of 1965, the section on to Tenbury having been demolished a little earlier. Without a rail link, all materials from the CM&DP had to be moved out by road. Telegraph poles were sold to a local riding school, fencing to local farmers, and most of the disused flat-bottom rail was sold for use in reinforcing sea defences on the East Coast. The culmination

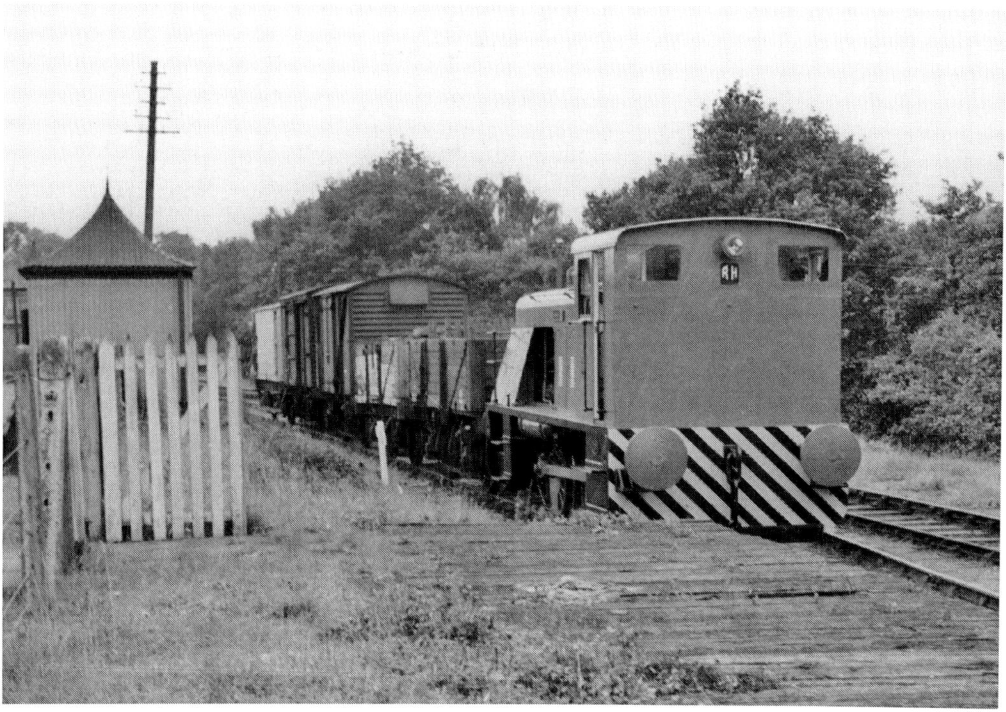

Cleobury Mortimer Junction with RNAD train, 31st August, 1962. *Author*

A view from the RNAD train at a crossing north of Prescott, 1962. *Author*

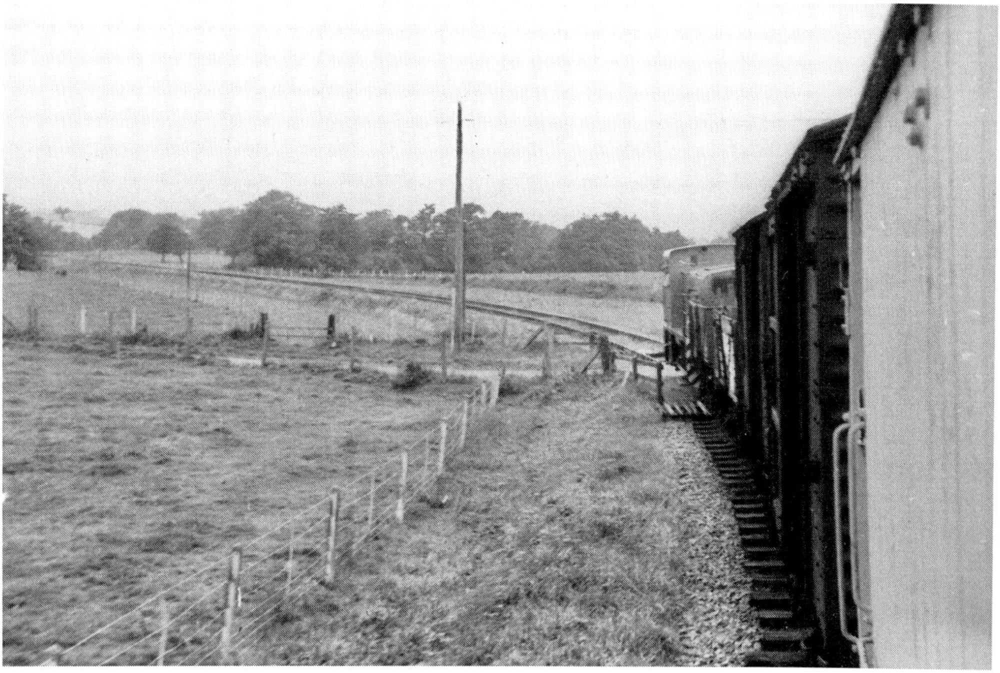

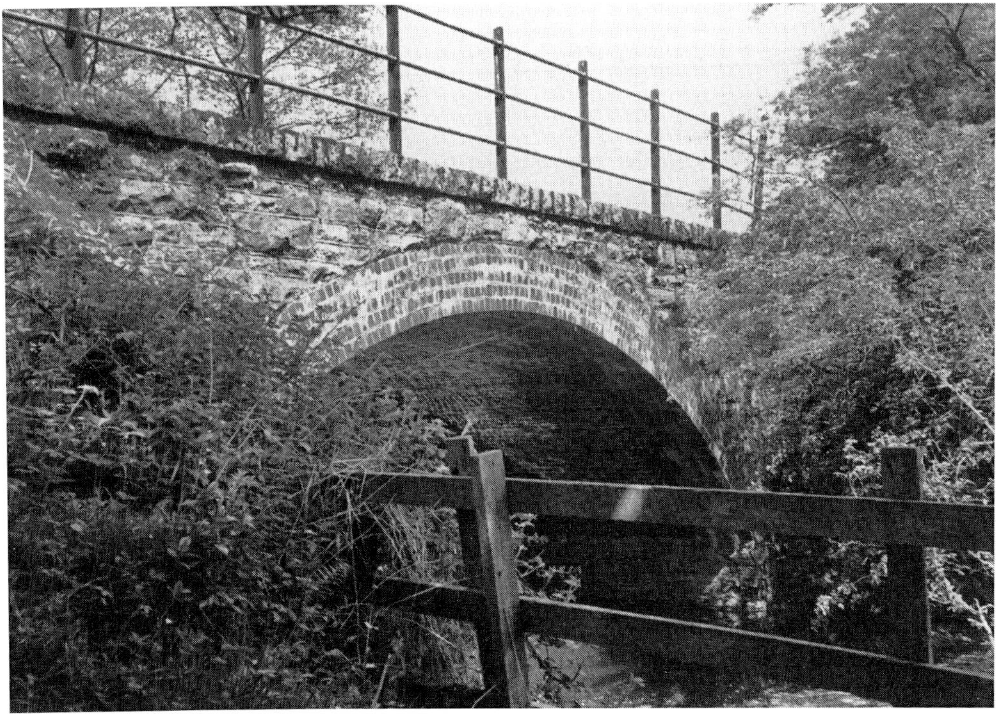

A typical CM&DPLR overbridge over the River Rea, Detton Ford, 1992. *Author*

CM&DP trackbed and site of Catherton Sidings, Detton Ford, 1992. *Author*

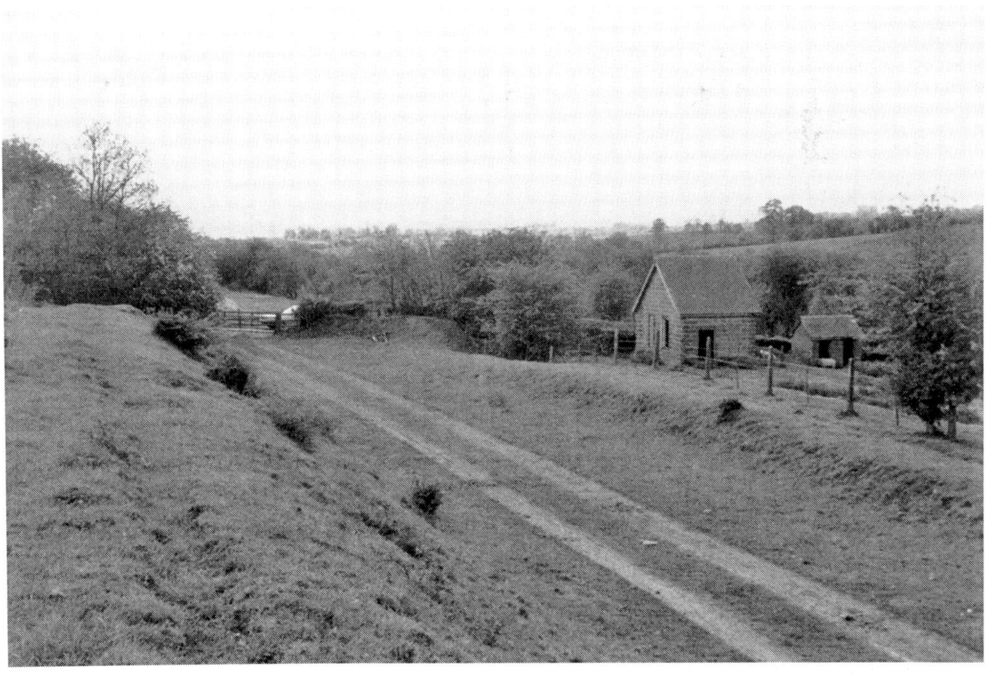

of the process was the sale of land to the adjoining landowners, the last conveyance being completed by the Department of the Environment's Property Services Agency in 1972.

The scene along the line in 1992 differed considerably from that in 1962. At that time it was still possible to report little change along the route: if anything, the track then was much less weedy than in some earlier days, although in many places flat-bottom rail had been replaced by chaired bullhead, set sometimes on concrete sleepers. In a few places some of the original track could still be seen. Not so now! Several stretches of the line have been ploughed back into the fields from which they were cut, and elsewhere the course of the railway has become heavily overgrown. The GWR station site at Cleobury Mortimer provides an instance of this, and by 1992 it was hard to believe that it had ever been a junction. Although the main building was standing, and in private occupation, the platforms were buried in spoil, and the signal box had vanished altogether. At the southern end of the station the goods yard and the site of the long abandoned siding provided for the Bayton Colliery Co. was occupied by caravans.

Fortunately it is still possible to see several relics of the CM&DP at Cleobury Town. The concrete office building is now a small bungalow, and the nearby station master's house is inhabited and apparently in good order. A dilapidated level crossing gate remains, as does an even more decayed concrete locomotive shed. It seems hard to credit now that in 1922 this structure achieved the status of being a sub-shed to Kidderminster. Nevertheless, it has survived so far in spite of disuse although the water tower and a wooden station shelter have gone.

The halt at Detton Ford also survives; the shelter was used as a store by a local smallholder for some years, but is now decaying. The site of the Catherton quarry sidings may still be identified adjacent to the railway, although at a slightly lower level, and a large slab of concrete marks the site of the stone crushing plant which was busy with traffic from the ropeway until the late 1920s or early 1930s. Incidentally, according to one of E.R. Calthrop's early plans, Detton Ford might have been called Detton Mill. On the same plan, Chilton was described as Neen Savage, and Prescott as Oreton. Although Neen Savage and Oreton were rather larger hamlets, their names did not prevail on the railway, and Prescott at least acquired moderate fame as the location of the line's largest civil engineering structure. That structure, the small viaduct over the Rea, still stands, but much of the trackbed nearby has disappeared under agriculture.

The wooden station building at Stottesdon has been demolished, and the site is occupied by a plantation of young trees. The site of the platform at Aston Botterell is marked by a low, grassy mound, but at Burwarton the platform edge is still visible in what is now a field for grazing horses. The dilapidated wooden station building at Burwarton was still standing until the early 1980s.

The scene at Cleobury North is rather different. Whereas in 1962 the small shelter still stood tidily on the low platform, by 1992 all traces of it had gone, and the trackbed for some distance north and south of the crossing was in use as a private road. About 150 yards north of the crossing, near the summit of the

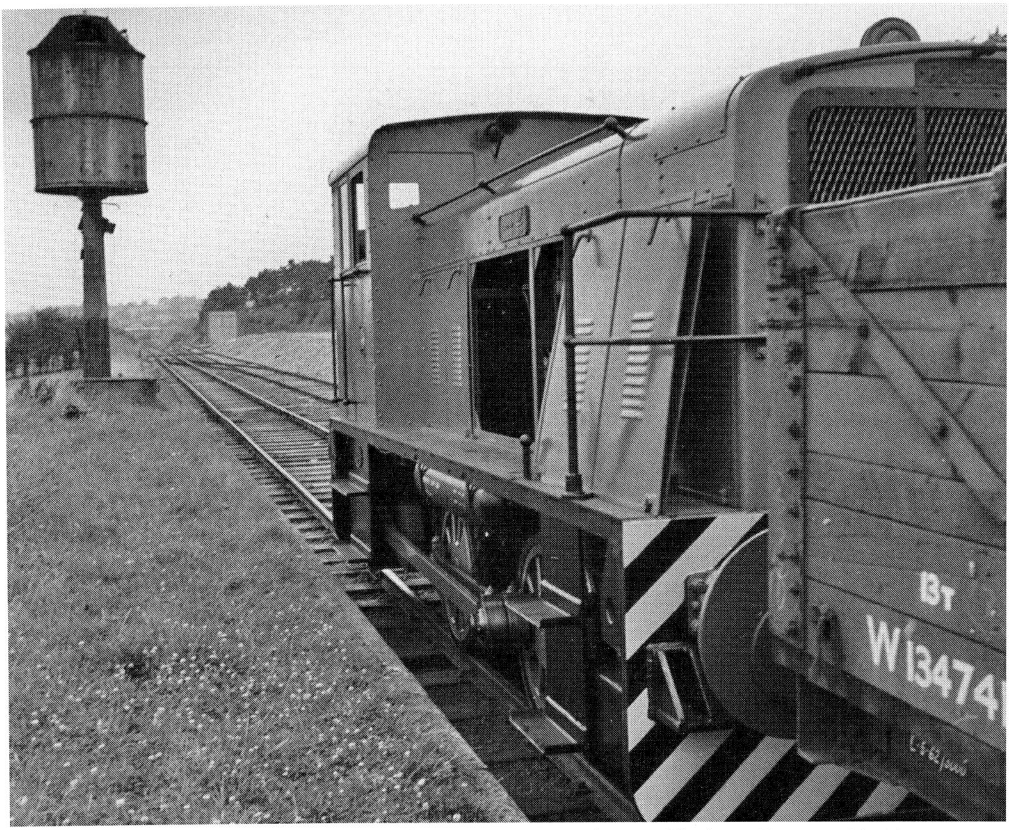

Ruston & Hornsby built RNAD diesel No. DP735 is seen here at Cleobury Town on 31st August, 1962. *Author*

A RNAD train seen near Cleobury North crossing, 1962. *Author*

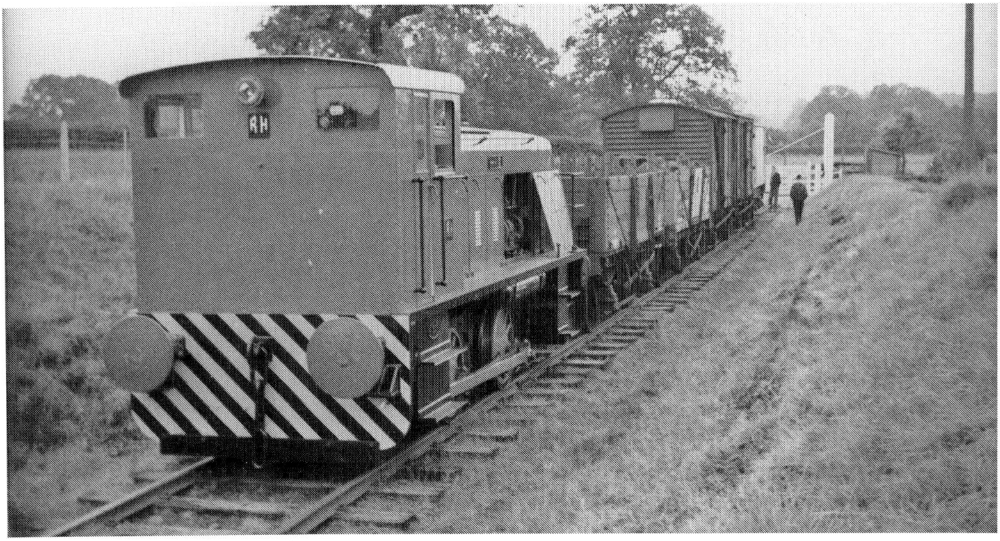

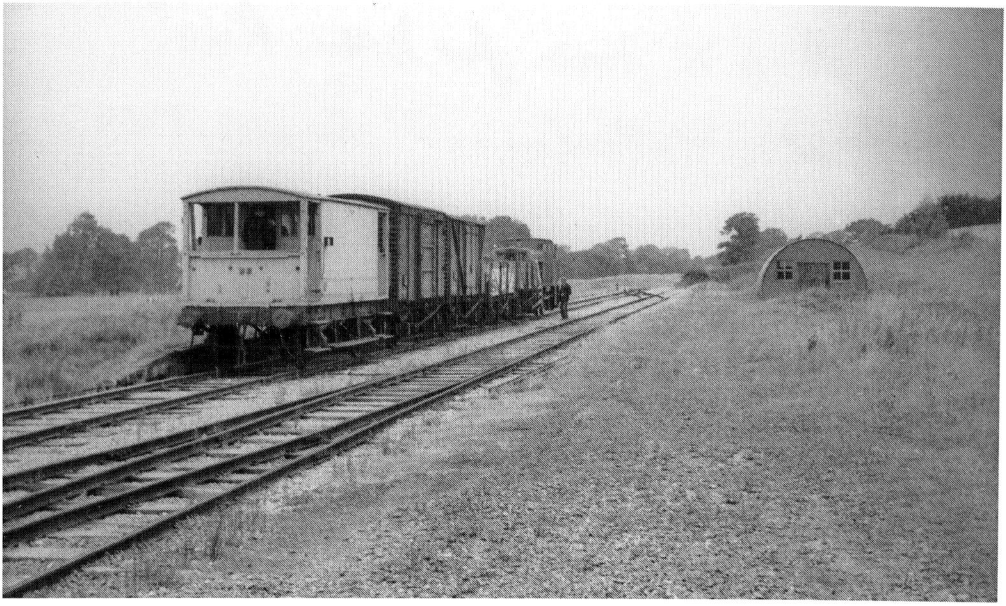

RNAD train for Ditton Priors halts at Stottesdon. *Author*

Cleobury Mortimer Junction station, from the fork between the CM&DP and the former GWR, August 1962. *Author*

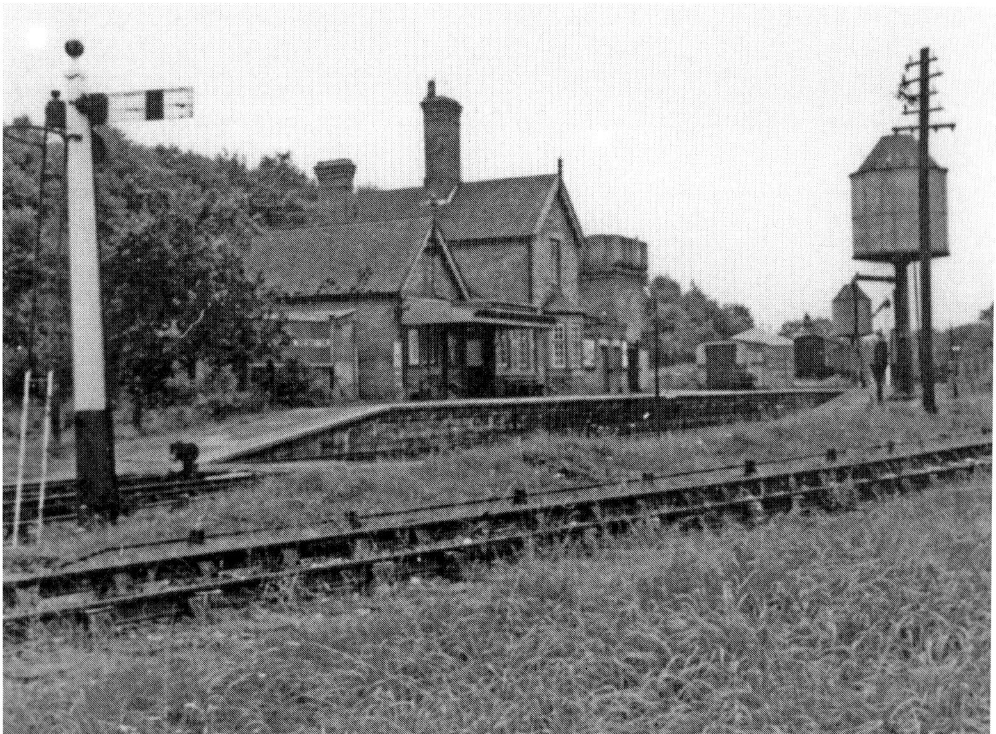

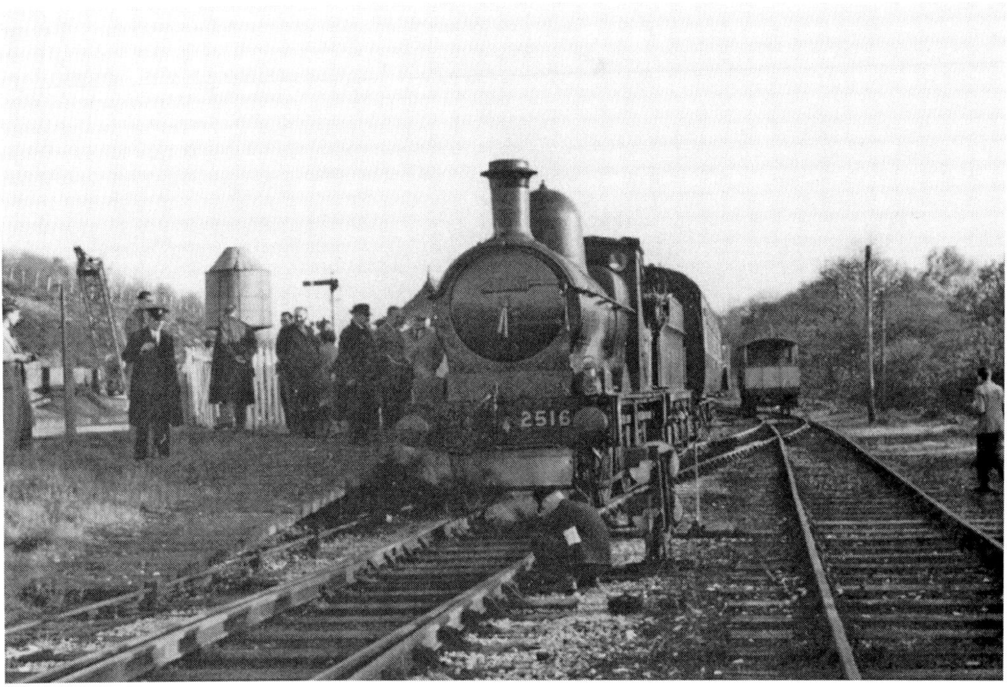

Ex-GWR 'Dean Goods' 0-6-0 No. 2516 at Cleobury Mortimer on an SLS Special, 21st May, 1955.
T.J. Edgington

On the same day ex-GWR 0-6-0PT No. 2144 is seen at Cleobury North. *T.J. Edgington*

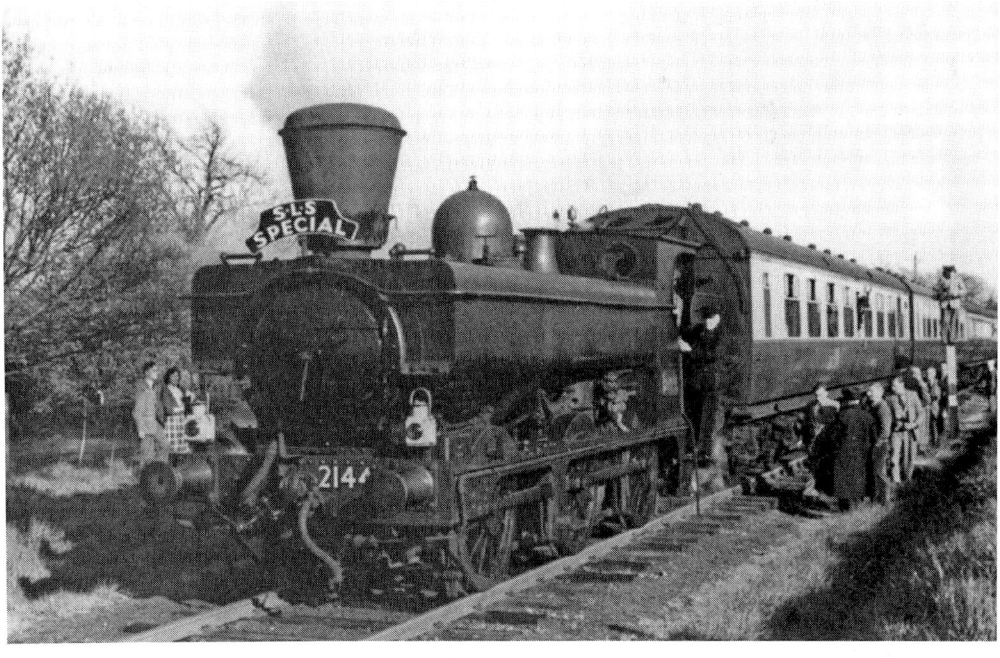

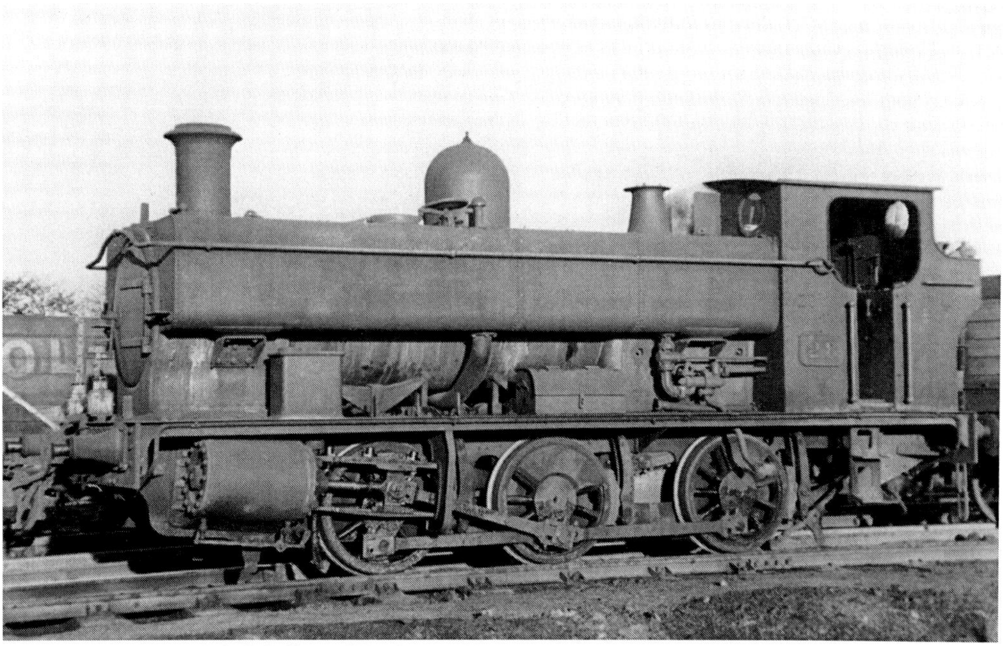

GWR No. 28 at Hafod Colliery, Wrexham, 1951. *R. Daniells Collection*

No. 29 with spark arrester at Kidderminster. *A.A.G. Delicata*

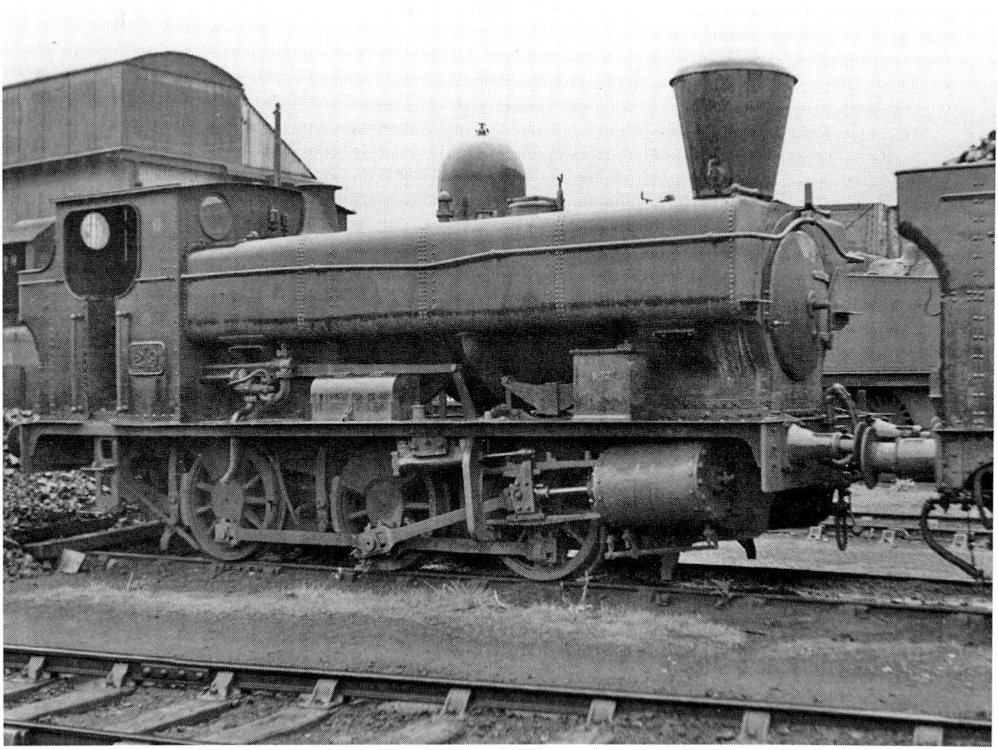

last 1 in 60 gradient, the trackbed widens at the point where, in World War II, an extra loop siding was installed on each side of the line to accommodate RNAD traffic. Although the railway and sidings have gone, in 1992 a WD pattern water crane survived, bearing the directions: 'Open and Shut 6 in. Valve'.

Although the RNAD has been closed for over a quarter of a century, many of the buildings of the depot remain - some derelict and some in use as part of the Ditton Priors trading estate. In 1974 the site of the railway terminus (apart from the RNAD locomotive shed) was cleared in anticipation of residential development. The station site is now occupied by homes, and the trackbed directly to the south has become a field. In 1992 it was hard to believe that the railway had ever reached Ditton Priors.

The best account of the CM&DPLR locomotives so far published is in Volume 10 of the Railway Correspondence and Travel Society history, *The Locomotives of the GWR*. Full details may be found there, but it may be of interest to note that as originally built, the engines had boilers measuring 9 ft 2 in. by 4 ft 1 in. by 4 ft 0 in., with 167 tubes of 1⅞ in. The total heating surface was 918.25 sq. ft the grate area 14.6 sq. ft and the tractive effort reckoned to be 18,240 lb. After rebuilding No. 29 (*Burwarton*) had a domed boiler of 9 ft 2 in. by 3 ft 10 in. by 3 ft 9⅛ in. with 207 1⅝ in. tubes, and a Belpaire firebox was fitted. The total heating surface was 909.57 sq. ft, and the grate area 14.7 sq. ft. The tank capacity was reduced to 850 gallons. This engine is thought to have acquired its large spark arrester in about 1939, but No. 28 is believed to have been so equipped only between 1944 and 1947.

Until 1938 the two engines continued their duties begun 30 years earlier, but, at the time the line closed to passengers, it was reported that *Burwarton* was nowhere to be seen. Certainly this locomotive was the first to wander, serving for spells at Worcester, Gloucester and Hereford. No. 28 was loaned to the NCB at Hafod Colliery, Wrexham, for a time in 1951, before moving to Swindon for store, and latterly Newport for shunting at Dock Street. No. 29 returned to Kidderminster in 1951, but was not given a great deal of exercise, as the CM&DP was by then usually worked by either Nos. 2101 or 2144, balloon-stacked 0-6-0PT's of the '2021' class. Even so, No. 29 did return to Ditton Priors a few times, and Tony Barfield, in his book *When there was Steam*, has given an entertaining railwayman's view of one of these trips on 'the Gadget', as the CM&DP line was sometimes known. The last steam locomotive (and the most modern) to work over the CM&DP regularly was '16XX' 0-6-0PT No. 1661. This engine, also fitted with a spark arrester, made its last trip in September 1957, just before the Admiralty took over. Some excellent pictures of No. 29 and the other pannier tanks which were at work on the railway at the period appear in G.F. Bannister s *Great Western Steam off the Beaten Track*.

The British Transport Records section of the Public Record Office contains a brief but interesting report on the CM&DPLR, made for the GWR in November 1921. At that time the Chairman of the light railway company was the Hon. Eustace S. Hamilton-Russell, of Stoke Lodge, Ludlow, and the other Directors were A.F. Bott, Kenneth C. Bayley and R.L. Caryl Roberts. The railway was said to comprise one mile of sidings and 12 miles of track, and the permanent way

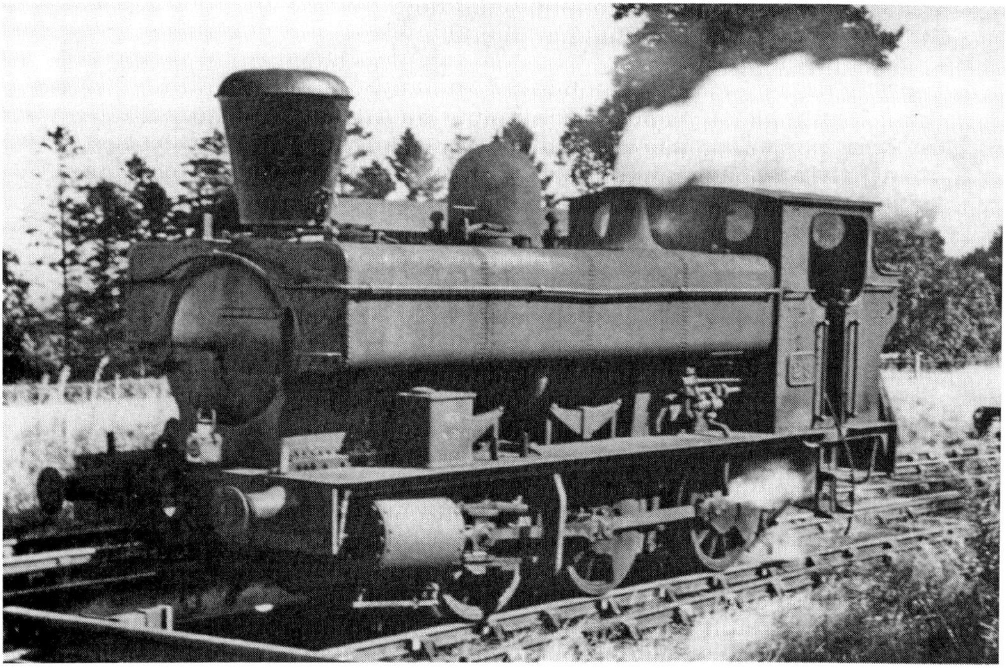

Another view of locomotive No. 29 with its spark arrester chimney. *R.C. Riley Collection*

Ex-GW 0-6-0PT No. 1661, the last steam locomotive to Ditton Priors, at Kidderminster, 1957. *R. Daniells*

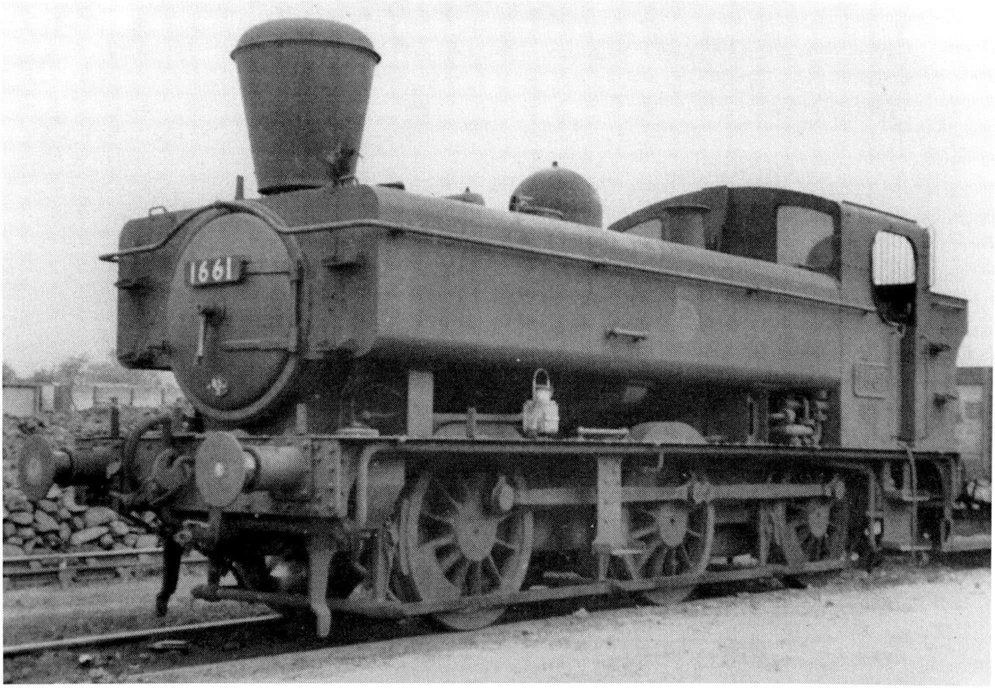

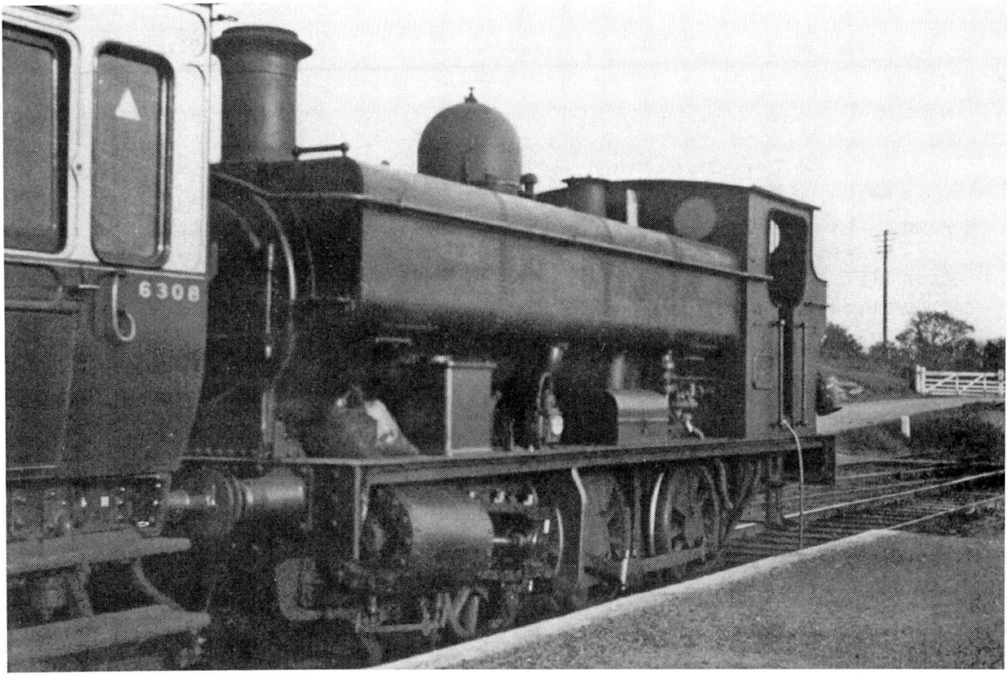

No. 28, at Cleobury Town on 11th May, 1935. *V.R. Webster*

Locomotive No. 28 is seen here stored at Kidderminster in August 1949.
K.J. Cooper Collection/Industrial Railway Society

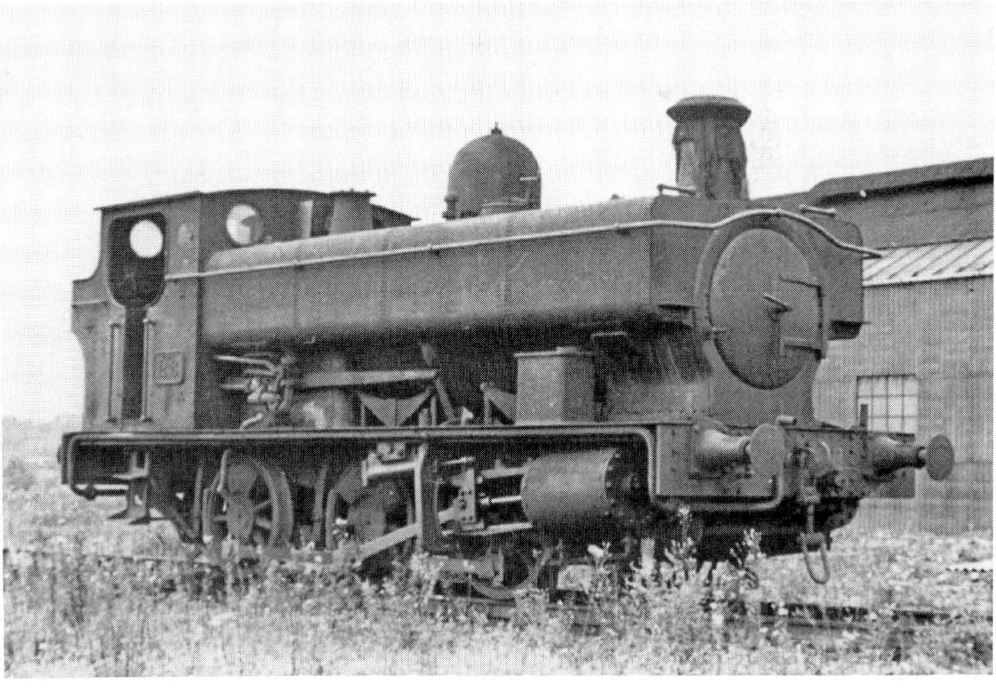

consisted of flat-bottom rails weighing 72 lb./yard. The axle loading was restricted to 14 tons under light railway regulations. The trainloads permitted were 12 trucks loaded with minerals, 17 with general goods, or 24 trucks empty. Irrespective of the official figures, it was reported in the *Locomotive Magazine* in June 1921 that 20 loaded stone wagons were taken up the 1 in 60 grades!

The report of November 1921 revealed quite an increase in traffic in 1920 over 1919. The figures for miles run in the two years are given below, and the growth in freight traffic is especially noticeable. Perhaps it was significant that by then a large quantity of stone was being taken by the GWR for ballasting!

Miles run in		*1919*		*1920*
Coaching		4,220		4,491
Freight		8,151		9,180
Shunting				
Coaching	690		992	
Freight	1,605		3,300	
		2,295		4,292
Assisting		72		136
		14,738		18,099

This was the Cleobury Mortimer and Ditton Priors Light Railway in its independent heyday. Although the railway has gone altogether now, a few relics have survived. One of the original North London coaches still exists as a grounded coach body close to the former Great Western main line at Challow, between Didcot and Swindon. For many years it saw use as a tiny Methodist chapel; in 1992 the gutted body served simply as a garden shed.

In the neighbourhood of Cleobury Mortimer, a complete CM&DP railwaymen's uniform is said to survive in private hands. The GWR Museum at Swindon has custody of the company seal. Apart from these items a modest amount of paperwork, and a number of tickets still survive. The rarity of the tickets means that the prices obtained when one comes onto the market would astonish anyone who knew the old line. Even now, though, the memory of the railway is valued in various ways, and it will surely never be forgotten in South Shropshire.

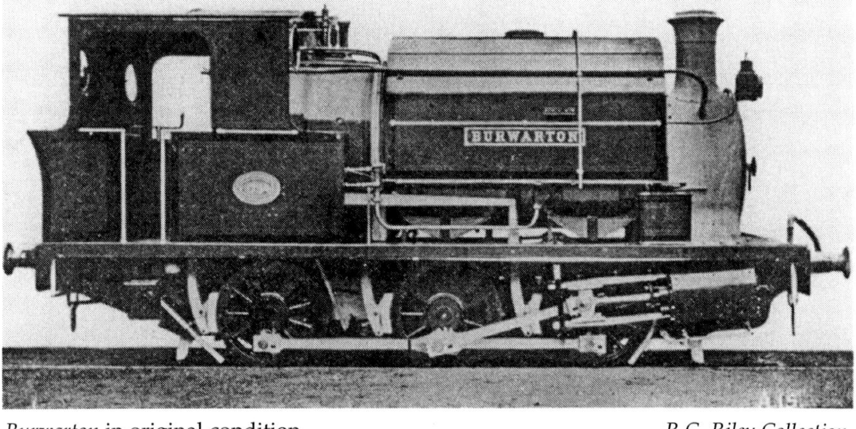

Burwarton in original condition. *R.C. Riley Collection*

Appendix One

Report of the Light Railway Commissioners to the Board of Trade, 1901

1. The application for an Order to authorise this light railway was made to the Commissioners by Viscount Boyne and Admiral Robert Woodward in May 1900.
2. The proposed railway is about 12¼ miles in length, wholly situate in the County of Salop and is to be constructed on the 4 ft 8½ in. gauge. It commences by a junction with the Great Western Railway (Tenbury and Bewdley Branch) near the existing Cleobury Mortimer Station, running thence past the villages of Cleobury Mortimer and Neen Savage and up the valley of the river Rea past Detton Mill and Oreton to Stottesden thence past Aston Botterell, Burwarton (the residence of Lord Boyne) and Cleobury North terminating at Ditton Priors.
   Lord Boyne and Admiral Woodward are the owners respectively of 5½ miles and 1¼ miles of the land through which the railway will run, and they have promoted this scheme with a view to opening up an agricultural district not served by any railway, and also said to be rich in minerals, including several stone quarries.
3. The Commissioners held a public inquiry at Cleobury Mortimer on the 18th October,1900, when all persons appearing before them were heard.
4. Mr Lloyd Baker who owns about 1¼ Miles of the land through which the railway will run objected on account of the severance of his arable fields and interference with his access to the river. In other respects the scheme was unanimously supported by representatives of all classes.
5. The Commissioners decided to grant the application considering that Mr Lloyd Baker's opposition was not of such a character as to outweigh the advantage to the public of the scheme. They therefore proceeded to settle provisionally the terms of their Order copies of the draft being sent to the Government Departments, to the Local Authorities and to persons interested for their observations.
6. It was stated at the local Inquiry that Lord Boyne intends to give his land for the railway, and to subscribe a considerable sum towards the undertaking: and further that his Lordship had already entered into communication with other landowners with the view of obtaining their lands for the purposes of the railway upon favourable terms. It was proposed by the Promoters in their draft Order that the Order should be granted to them personally and that they should be in a position to transfer it (with any lands or any other rights or property acquired as aforesaid, but without profit to themselves) to some 'Syndicate' who would find the rest of the Capital and work the Railway. The Commissioners considered that this course would be unusual and would present some difficulties. They have therefore recommended the Promoters to make arrangements for giving effect to their intentions outside the Order; and the Order will incorporate a Company, of which Mr Hamilton Russell (Lord Boyne's son) and two representatives of the Syndicate in question are to be nominated as the first Directors. The names of the latter should be submitted to the Board of Trade before the Order is finally confirmed.
7. The material points arising upon the Commissioners' draft Order to which their attention has been called are as follows:-

   On behalf of the Promoters it was submitted:-

   (a) That the qualification of Directors should be not less than £350 in the share capital of the Company.

The Commissioners have made this amendment.

(b) That the Capital of the Company should be increased from £96,000 to £100,000. The Commissioners have carefully reconsidered the Estimate in connection with this point. They think the estimate a liberal one and that a share capital of £96,000 with borrowing powers gives an ample margin for all purposes.

It will be observed that in Clause 39 an increase of 20 per cent over main line goods rates is authorised, having been asked for by the Promoters. If the expected development of mineral traffic is realised such increased rate may become unnecessary and would be reduced accordingly after the period of 5 years by the Board of Trade. In the opinion of the Commissioners it is not probable that the mineral capabilities of the district would be opened up and developed so as to produce that effect in any less period; and in this case as in other previous cases they do not think that the reasons for allowing a special rate would be affected by the transfer of the light railway to an existing railway company.

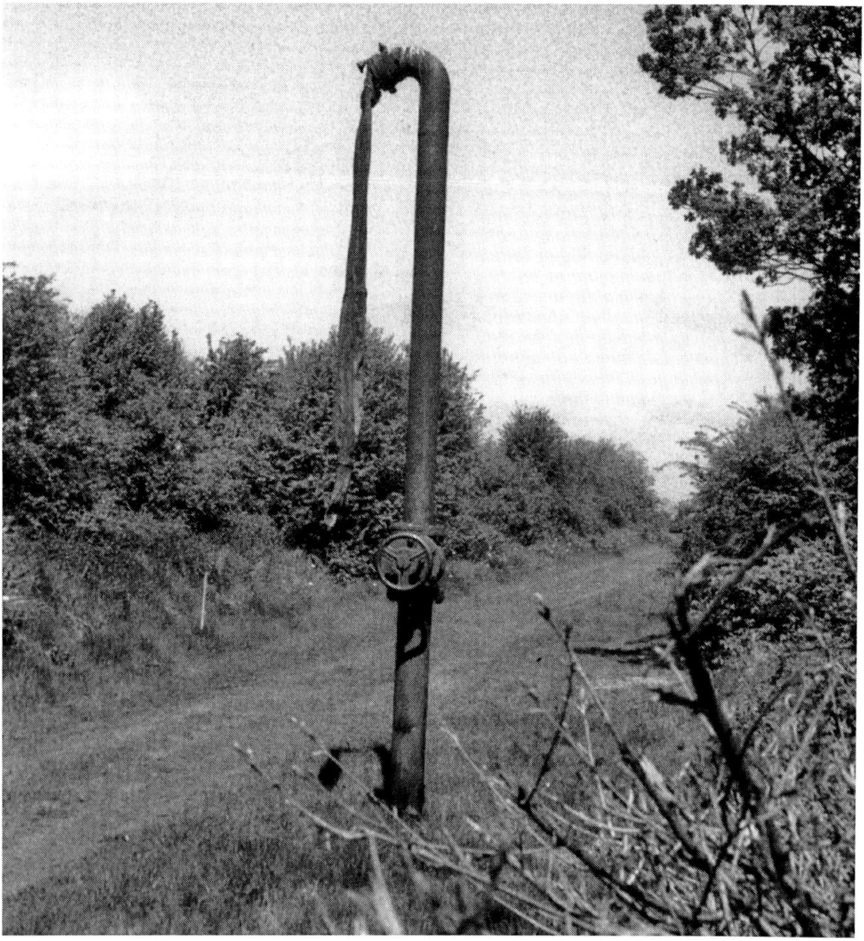

Former WD water crane at the site of the exchange sidings, near Cleobury North, 1992.
Author

Appendix Two

Report of Col H.A. Yorke, Inspecting Officer, to the Board of Trade

RAILWAY DEPARTMENT

BOARD OF TRADE
8 Richmond Terrace,
Whitehall, London, S.W.

Sir,

16th November, 1908.

I have the honour to report for the information of the Board of Trade that in compliance with the instructions contained in your Minute of the 4th November, I inspected on the 13th instant the Cleobury Mortimer & Ditton Priors Light Railway, authorised by the Order of 1901.

The railway commences by a junction with the Great Western Rly at Cleobury Mortimer station, and terminates at Ditton Priors. The length of the line is 12 m. 0.67 chs. The gauge is 4 ft. 8½ in., and the motive power is steam. The line is single throughout, and sidings have been constructed at the stations and at certain intermediate places.

The gradients are numerous and severe, the worst being 1 in 60. The curves are also very numerous, the sharpest having a radius of 10 chains, except at the junction with the Great Western Rly, where there is a curve a few yards in length with a radius of 6 chains.

The permanent way is constructed with secondhand flat bottomed rails weighing about 72 lb. per yard, which are secured to the sleepers by dog spikes and fang bolts and clips, the fang bolts being placed on each side of the rails at the joints and also on the outside of each rail half-way between the joints. On curves, additional fang bolts are used on the outside of the outer rail, and this rail is further supported on the outside by blocks of wood spiked to the sleepers and pressing against the web of the rail. The sleepers are 8 feet long by 9 in. by 42 in. The ballast consists of broken stone and furnace ashes. I noticed in many places a deficiency of ballast, which should be made good as soon as possible.

The road bed is not yet thoroughly consolidated and, having regard to the class of engine which is to be used upon the line, viz. a six-wheeled-coupled tank engine, weighing 39 tons - or 13 tons per axle - the line will have to be carefully watched and maintained, and I recommend that for the first six months the speed should nowhere exceed 20 miles an hour, in place of the 25 miles an hour authorised by the Order.

There are 8 bridges under the line, all constructed with brick arches resting upon masonry or concrete abutments. All the bridges appeared to be standing well, and showed no sign of movement.

There are ten level-crossings of the railway over Parish roads, and three over turnpike roads. The level-crossings over the Parish roads are not provided with gates, but with cattle guards, notices, and speed boards, in accordance with the Order. Of the level-crossings of turnpike roads, one is provided with cattle guards, and the other two with gates, which are kept closed across the railway. One of the latter is not near a station, and there is no-one available for opening and closing the gates; the Company therefore desire the permission of the Board of Trade that the opening and closing of the gates shall be performed by the guard or fireman of each train, in accordance with Section 23 sub-section 4(a) of the Order.

There are four stations on the railway, viz: Ditton Priors, Burwarton, Stottesdon and

Cleobury Town, besides Cleobury Mortimer Junction station (which is the property of the Great Western Rly, and as to which a separate report will be made). The stations on the Light Railway each consist of a short platform, one foot above rail level, and the carriages to be used upon the railway are fitted with steps to enable passengers conveniently to enter or leave the trains. The platform at Cleobury Mortimer Junction station is, however, of the usual standard height, namely three feet, and care will have to be taken that the steps referred to clear the high platform at the junction. Unfortunately the steps were not fitted to the carriages at the time of my inspection, and I was not therefore able to see whether they were suitable for both high and low platforms. At each station a small shelter has been provided, and also name boards and lamps. The issuing and collecting of tickets will, I understand, be carried out by the guard of the train.

The line is to be worked as one section by one engine in steam, or two engines coupled together, carrying a train staff. And an undertaking to this effect, under the Seal of the Company, has already been forwarded to the Board of Trade. There are therefore no signals on the line, except at the junction with the Great Western Rly at Cleobury Mortimer.

There are siding connections at all the stations and at four intermediate points. The connections at the intermediate sidings are worked by single lever ground frames, locked by the key on the train staff, the points being fitted with the usual safety appliances. But the connections at the stations are worked by ordinary balance levers, and are merely secured by padlocks. This is not satisfactory, and the arrangements at the stations should be made similar to those at the intermediate sidings, viz. the points should be worked by levers locked by the train staff, and the points on the main line should have the usual safety appliances. This alteration should be carried out within three months.

Subject to the conditions mentioned above, viz. (a) that the ballasting should be completed as soon as possible, (b) that the speed for the first six months should not exceed 20 miles an hour, and (c) that the siding connections at the stations shall be controlled by the key on the train staff, I can recommend the Board of Trade to sanction the use of this Light Railway.

I understand that the proposed service on the railway is three trains each way daily, the whole of which the Company propose to run as mixed trains.

(Signed) H.A.YORKE

THE CLEOBURY MORTIMER AND DITTON PRIORS LIGHT RAILWAY COMPANY HEREBY UNDERTAKE THAT so long as the Railway between Cleobury Mortimer and Ditton Priors consists of a single line only, such Railway shall be worked:

(a) With only one engine in steam or two or more engines coupled together upon the single line or any section thereof at one and the same time. Such engine or engines to carry the staff belonging to the line or section on which the train is travelling.*

GIVEN UNDER THE SEAL OF THE CLEOBURY MORTIMER AND DITTON PRIORS LIGHT RAILWAY COMPANY this Fourth day of November 1908.

Signed: S. GORE BROWNE Chairman

A. PHILLIPS Secretary

* N.B. No tickets to be allowed under this mode of working.

Appendix Three

Meetings and Correspondence Concerning Absorption

CONFIDENTIAL

RAILWAYS ACT, 1921

CLEOBURY MORTIMER & DITTON PRIORS LIGHT RAILWAY COMPANY

Memorandum of Meeting held at Paddington on the 10th January, 1922.

Present

Cleobury Mortimer & Ditton Priors Light Railway Company.	Great Western Company.
Mr Morris	Mr Bolter Mr Hubbard Mr Showers

It was agreed that the net receipts of 1913 would be the basis of settlement of terms of absorption of the Light Railway.

The net receipts for 1913 amounted to £3068.

The capital is :-

£27, 000 Loans.

Mr Morris said these were held by the Viscount Boyne. Although shewn in the accounts as bearing interest at 5 per cent, he said Lord Boyne was as a matter of fact accepting 4 per cent. He will ascertain and let us know what are the conditions as regards repayment.

£87,051 Ordinary Shares.

These are mainly held by the Boyne family and their connections. The dividend paid in 1920 was 1½ per cent per annum.

There is a debit balance on Capital Account of £5,642, but as against this there is a revenue balance carried forward which on the 31st December, 1920 was £11,107.

Mr Morris said that the principal traffic over the line was roadstone. Owing to its high cost, the demand for this had fallen off during the last few months, but he is quite satisfied that the business in this stone will soon recover.

He will send detailed particulars of the Light Railway Company's Accounts for 1920.

As to terms, he said he was sure there should be no difficulty. The question appears to be whether, if the Loans be permanently fixed at 4 per cent, the Ordinary Stock should be exchanged for Great Western Ordinary Stock on a 1½ per cent or 2 per cent dividend basis, and to what extent the carry forward should pass to the Great Western Company after discharging the overdraft on Capital Account.

Mr Morris was disposed to agree that any monies coming to the Light Railway Company out of the £60,000,000 Government compensation should pass to the Great Western Company.

It was left that he would send the particulars required and that the General Manager would arrange for a representative to meet Mr Morris and go over the Cleobury Mortimer Company's Line, after which a further meeting could be arranged no doubt to settle the terms for absorption.

RAILWAYS ACT, 1921
CLEOBURY MORTIMER & DITTON PRIORS LIGHT RAILWAY

Notes of Meeting held at Paddington on Thursday, February 9th 1922

PRESENT:-

Mr Pole
Mr Bolter
Mr Cope
Mr Hubbard
Mr Showers

The Hon. E.S. Hamilton-Russell
Mr K.C. Bayley
Mr C.E. Morris

Reference was made to the discussion which took place with Mr Morris on January 10th and the Light Railway Company's Accounts for 1921, which had since been furnished by that gentleman, were examined.
As a result of discussion it was agreed to recommend that the absorption of the Light Railway Company's undertaking in the Great Western Company should be on the following basis:-

Light Railway Co.'s Stock	*Great Western Company's Stock to be issued in exchange*
£27,000 Loans	£27,000 4 per cent Debenture Stock
£87,051 Ordinary Shares	£29,017 Consolidated Ordinary Stock.

All reserves of the Light Railway Company, including sums received or receivable out of the £60,000,000 compensation payable by the Government, and surplus revenue accruing for the year 1921 after payment of interest at 4 per cent on Loans and Dividend at the rate of 1½ per cent on Ordinary Shares, to pass to Great Western Company.

Compensation to Directors for loss of Office to be paid out of the assets of the Light Railway Company on the basis of four years' fees understood to be £100 per annum.

The arrangement to take effect as from January 1st, 1922 and to be included in a Preliminary Scheme of Absorption which it was intimated on behalf of the Great Western Company would shortly be prepared.

Mr Bayley intimated that he represented the interests of Lord Boyne who had advanced the £27,000 shewn as Loans in the Light Railway Company's Accounts. Although this loan was bearing interest at 4 per cent it had been made on the basis of 5 per cent and Lord Boyne had looked for the repayment of the capital within a few years. Mr. Bayley intimated that he could not, therefore, definitely commit Lord Boyne to the acceptance of 4 per cent GW Debenture Stock but he would be approached in the matter.

It was stated that the Registered Office of the Light Railway Company was at 116 Victoria Street, S.W., where certain clerical work was performed at a cost of about £200 per annum, and it was intimated on behalf of the Great Western Company that no objection would be raised on their part to compensation on the basis of one year's expenses being paid to Mr Bott (a Director of the Company and at whose Offices the work was performed) in respect of the discontinuance of these services.

Mr Morris enquired as to his personal position when the absorption took place. He stated that he was 59 years of age and his salary was £600 per annum. He had been General Manager of the Light Railway since it was opened in 1908 and had previously been in the service of the Metropolitan Company. His terms of service included a pension payable by the Light Railway Company on retirement. Mr Pole said that Mr Morris, with the other staff of the Light Railway, would be transferred to the Great Western service on conditions not less favourable than those they now enjoy, and any obligation entered into by the Light Railway Company as to the payment of a pension to their General Manager on retirement would be assumed by Great Western Company. It was arranged that details of this obligation would be furnished formally to the Great Western Company.

List of Shareholders

Name	*Number of Shares*
R.L. Caryl Roberts	250
T.D. Munns	250
The Hon. F.G. Hamilton Russell	250
E.R. Calthrop	50
David Marcus	25
G.F. Polglasse	25
J.J. Winn	25
Thomas Williams	25
John Adams	20
Sir William B. Peat	1
R.B. Petre	1
Exors. of E.G. Marshall	250
E.S. Hamilton Russell	5,316
S. Gore Brown	661
The Hon. Claude Hamilton Russell	5,000
G.D. Gibson	450
E.T. Foxlee	6
G.F. Grover	150
W.A. Ellis	475
R. Lee Roberts	50
T.L. Roberts	50
Excess Insurance Company	1,193
W.C. Stennett	11,219
Railway & General Dev. Co.	200
The Right Hon. Viscount Boyne	29,195
S.L. Hunt	105
Hudson Matthews & Co.	250
The Hon. Arthur Hamilton Russell	5,000
F.B. Howse	198
A.F. Bott	24,866
Hamish Cross	726
Mrs Cleaver	119
Burwarton Coal & Trading Co,	400
K.C. Bayley	250
	87,051

Cleobury Mortimer & Ditton Priors
Light Railway,
Cleobury Mortimer

M.321

10th March 1922

Dear Sir,

Railways Act 1921.

Referring to conversation with you on the 1st instant, I have pleasure in advising you that at a Board Meeting of this Company held on the 28th ultimo my Directors agreed to the terms for the absorption of this Railway suggested at the meeting held at Paddington on the 9th ultimo, a copy of the minutes of that meeting having already been received from your Office.

I would point out, however, that in the third paragraph of the first page it is stated that 1½ per cent Dividend should be paid, whereas at the meeting it was agreed that 2 per cent should be paid on our Ordinary Shares for 1921. I have already mentioned this verbally, and perhaps you will kindly confirm.

As regards the last paragraph, it is understood that this does not quite meet the case, and that you are writing me further on the subject as promised.

With reference to the surplus revenue accruing up to the end of 1921 after payment of Interest at 4 per cent on £27,000 Loan, and Dividend at 2 per cent on Ordinary Shares, it is proposed by my Board of Directors that the following amounts should be paid in respect of compensation, etc.:-

Directors	- On the basis of four years fees, viz. £100 per annum.	£400
Mr A.F. Bott	- In respect of Office at 116 Victoria Street and clerical work performed at a cost of £200 per annum - one year's expenses.	£200
Mr E.J. Morris	- General Manager - grant for special services performed during Government Control.	£100
		£700

I trust that this will be satisfactory to you, and perhaps you will kindly advise me in due course.

Yours faithfully,

E.J. MORRIS

CLEOBURY MORTIMER & DITTON PRIORS LIGHT RAILWAY

E.J. MORRIS
General Manager

GENERAL MANAGER'S OFFICE,
CLEOBURY MORTIMER, SALOP

M.321

13th March, 1922

Dear Sir,

RAILWAYS ACT, 1921.
Cleobury Mortimer & Ditton Priors Light Railway.
Proposed Absorption Scheme.

Referring to your letter of the 8th instant addressed to 116 Victoria Street, which I have now received together with draft of the Absorption Scheme giving effect to the terms agreed with this Company, I may say that following a later interview with Mr Pole, a letter was sent to that gentleman on the 10th instant intimating that my Directors had agreed to the terms for the absorption of this Railway suggested at the meeting held at Paddington on the 9th ultimo. There were, however, *two minor questions* raised in my letter concerning which I am waiting your Company's reply.

With these exceptions there do not appear to be any points calling for further discussion, and I shall be glad to receive in due course the notice for insertion in the newspapers, and the circular and form of proxy mentioned in the last paragraph of your letter.

My Chairman suggests that our meeting should be held on Tuesday, 4th April, if possible, and I trust this will be satisfactory.

Yours faithfully,

(Signed)
E.J. MORRIS

A.E.Bolter Esq.,
Great Western Railway,
Paddington

CM&DPLR Receipts 1913-1919

Year	*Nett* £	*Ordinary Dividend* %	*Carry Forward* £
1913	3,069	*	2,998
1914	2,816	*	4,734
1915	2,822	*	6,476
1916	2,747	*	8,143
1917	3,122	*	10,185
1918	2,724	1½	10,523
1919	2,491	1½	10,632

* Interest on loans paid at the rate of 4%

Statement of Capital as at 31st December 1919: -

Ordinary Stock	£86,792
Loans @ 5%	27,000
Capital Account Debit Balance	4,283
Reserve Account	664

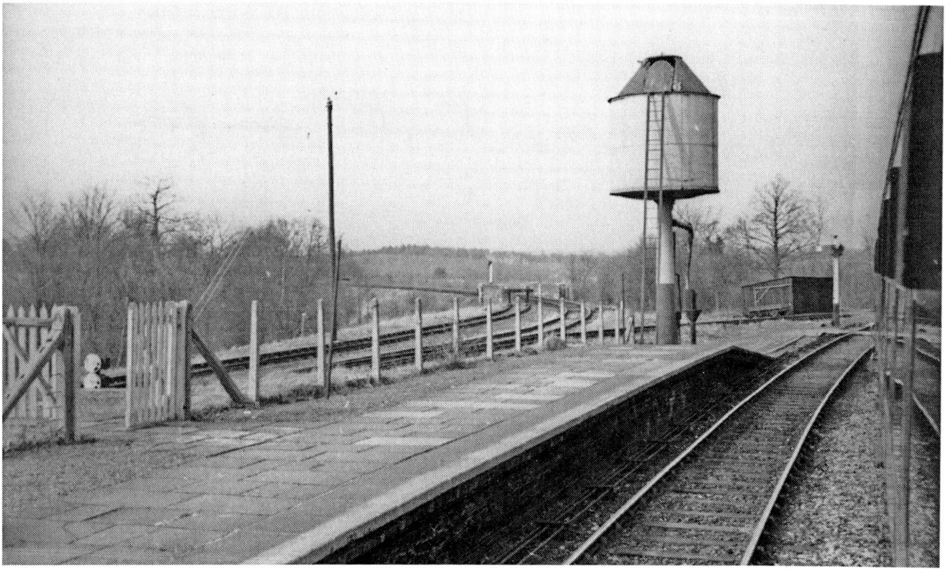

Cleobury Mortimer Junction, seen from a Bewdley – Tenby Wells train on 24th April, 1962. The CM&DP line can be seen curving away in the distance. *M.R.C. Price*

The station building and platform at Burwarton on 31st August, 1962. The track maintenance gang were having a bonfire beyond – hence smoke obscuring the track. *M.R.C. Price*

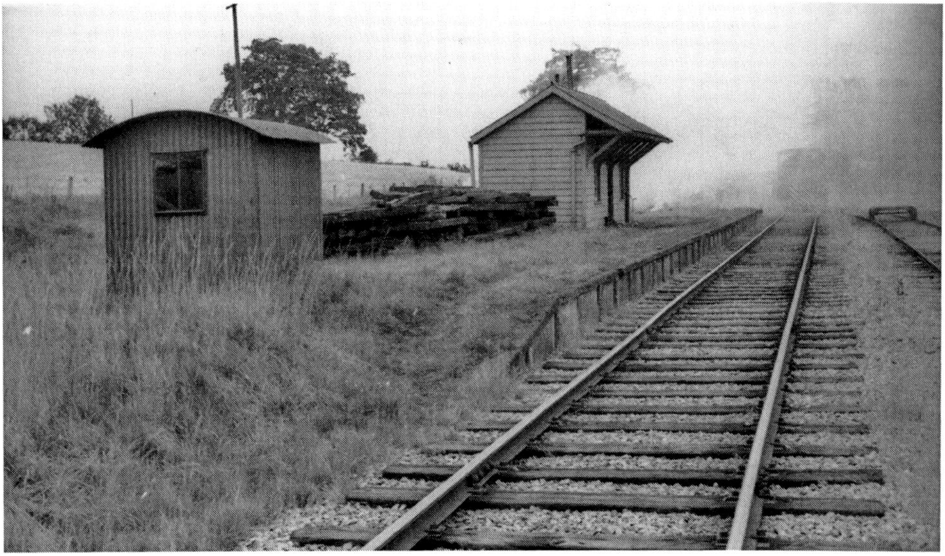

The Ludlow and Clee Hill Railway

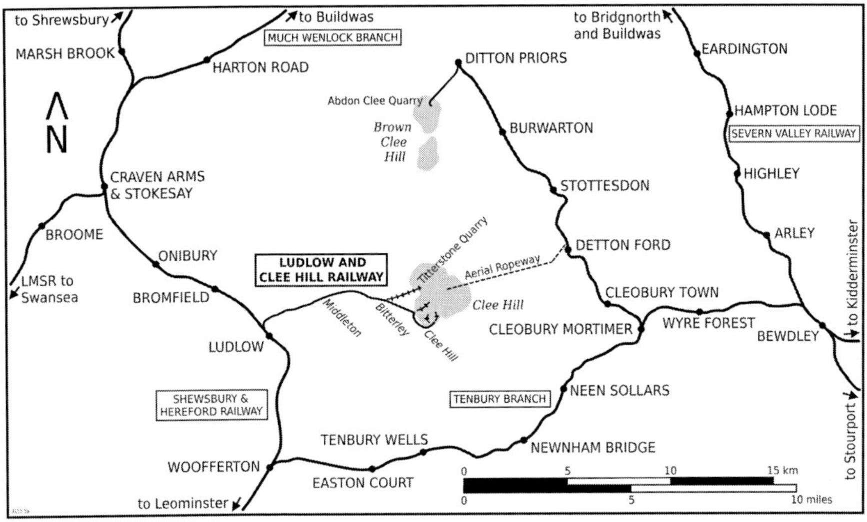

The Cleobury Mortimer & Ditton Priors Light Railway was not the only, nor even the earliest railway to be built to exploit the various minerals of the Clee Hills. Whilst the Abdon Clee Company worked the dolerite or "dhu stone" on the Abdon Burf area of Brown Clee Hill, in the nineteenth century development was concentrated on the more southerly Titterstone Clee, and the adjoining Clee Hill, both of which were over 1,600 feet high. In comparison with less elevated parts of south Shropshire, the weather in this exposed area was – and is – notoriously fickle, with strong winds, drizzle, and frequent fogs. Although only five or six miles east of the historic market town of Ludlow, the Clee Hills were (and some say, still are) a place apart, inhabited by a tough, resourceful and self-reliant working population. Rarely prosperous, these folk were well used to walking miles to and from work at the start and the end of the day, and their distinctive lifestyle was reflected in their use of a local dialect and vocabulary. As these hills held outcrops of iron ore, coal and limestone, as well as dhu stone, many men worked in the extractive industries. However, the main business was working the dhu stone, a material so hard that quarrying it was always known to be an especially gruelling occupation.

Although the commercial potential of the various minerals had been recognised by the middle of the nineteenth century, it was the dramatic expansion of Cardiff docks to serve the coal trade in the 1850's which first encouraged the use of Clee Hill stone outside the immediate district. Inadequate transport facilities had inhibited commercial development for generations, but the opening of the Shrewsbury & Hereford Railway in 1855, creating a connection with other railways into South Wales, effectively reduced the problem to one of conveying stone down from the quarries to the railway at Ludlow. The logical next step was to build another railway towards the quarries, and in July, 1861 an Act was passed for the construction of the Ludlow & Clee Hill Railway. This was proposed as a branch line, running over four miles eastwards from the Shrewsbury & Hereford Railway at Ludlow, to the small village of Bitterley, at the foot of the Titterstone and Clee Hills.

As the essential purpose of the railway was to convey minerals, no provision was ever made for passengers. The line was built from Clee Hill Junction, just north of Ludlow, and climbed steadily towards Middleton Siding (at 2 miles 24 chains), which was intended for general goods. The rails then continued up to Bitterley (4 miles 28 chains), where the final half mile was laid on a vicious 1 in 20 gradient. Such was the severity of this bank that it was soon recognised that eastbound trains would have to be divided at Middleton Siding, before being worked forward to Bitterley as two separate trains. In due course trains between Ludlow and Middleton included two brakevans – one at the rear in the usual way, and the other in the middle of the train at the point where it was to be divided. The L.&C.H.R. opened as a private railway on 24th August, 1864, although by then plans were well in hand for an extension of another 1 ½ miles, including a huge cable-worked incline to lift the railway up to Clee Hill Top.

By the time the L&CHR opened for traffic, the Shrewsbury & Hereford Railway had been included in a joint Great Western/ London & North Western Railway operating agreement of 1862. The L&CHR was not fully vested in their Joint Committee until 1893, but from the completion of the extension on 1 June, 1867, it was worked under an agreement with that body. The new extension promptly gained a remarkable claim to fame, because the incline was the longest standard gauge self-acting cable-worked incline anywhere in the British Isles. Like the Abdon Clee incline at Ditton Priors, the Clee Hill incline looked ferocious, but officially was graded at 1 in 9 over much of the 1,988 yards, although steepening to 1 in 6 near the summit. The cable was actually a wire rope, of 4 ½ in. circumference, and at the top it passed around a drum and a grooved guide wheel in the tall brick-built winding house, which was situated just below the main quarry of the Clee Hill Dhu Stone Company. Alongside the winding house there were several sidings, including one which specifically served the adjacent quarry. To add to the interest at this

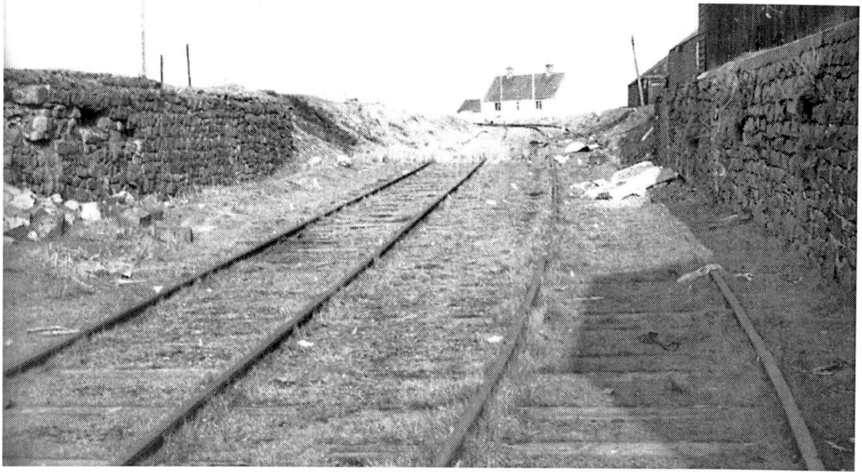

The clearly Ludlow & Clee Hill Railway at Clee Hill Goods in April, 1962. M.R.C. Price

location, the quarry company had a short but quite separate 3′ gauge tramway incline to bring stone down to a tipping area just above this standard gauge siding.

A very early and spectacular runaway on the standard gauge incline fortunately caused no fatalities, although it did cause considerable damage at Bitterley. Thereafter the rules for operating the incline were refined and strictly enforced, a warning bell and signalling system being installed to maintain understanding between the men working at the top and the bottom. As with many other self-acting inclines, there was a passing loop at the mid-point to allow ascending and descending wagons to pass, but the most unusual feature of this particular incline was the provision of three rails on the upper section (the central rail being used in common) and only a conventional two rails on the lower section. Freight wagons were not directly connected to the haulage rope, but rather a drawbar hook on the underside of a "dummy" brake vehicle – a suitably strengthened open wagon fitted with a hand brake. These were always positioned at the lower end of each "trip" of wagons on the incline, thereby protecting that trip from any possible breakaways. In later years the maximum permitted number of descending (loaded) wagons was five, with a weight not exceeding 85 tons, whilst the number of ascending (mostly empty) wagons varied according to their weight, and weather conditions – wet rails being more hazardous. The operating instructions asserted emphatically that a locomotive should never be used to give a push start to a descending trip of wagons.

At the outset the L&CHR acquired 0-6-0WT (Sharp Stewart 1477 of 1863), which was employed initially between Ludlow and Bitterley. It was named "Sir Charles", after Sir Charles Rouse-Boughton, a prominent local landowner and investor in the Clee Hill works. It is believed that for about ten years from 1867 rail movements on the railway above the main incline were handled by horses. By 1877, though, "Sir Charles" had been hauled up the incline and put to work between the quarries. Soon after a timber-built engine shed, with adjacent water tank, was erected about 150 yards beyond the incline top. The location chosen was so exposed to wind and weather that the shed eventually had to be buttressed by four massive baulks of timber to support and strengthen each side. In the 1890's "Sir Charles" was taken into L&NWR stock as No.1189, and later replaced by a small L&NW 0-4-0ST, No.3243. A fine photograph still exists of this saddle tank shunting wagons in the Dhu Stone quarry siding alongside the winding house. Once the L&CHR became the responsibility of the GWR/LNWR Joint Committee the modest Clee Hill shed became a sub-shed to Shrewsbury, and maintenance of the line was entrusted to the GWR Engineer's Department at Shrewsbury. In 1911 they came up with the idea of using tallow to lubricate the winding drum, and the outcome was said to be a quite remarkable improvement in the life of the brake blocks – from about 15 days to maybe 6 years! Unfortunately this report does not make clear how the tallow actually achieved such a spectacular result.

The Clee Hill Dhu Stone Company has been mentioned, but at the very end of the branch, over six miles from Ludlow, there were quarries belonging to the Clee Hill Granite Company. Their quarries also included the Magpie Quarry, a short distance to the north, which dispatched stone by aerial ropeway over Catherton Common down to Detton Ford on the CM&DPLR. This same company also had some commercial association with the Clee Hill Mining & Development Company, a small coal mining concern with an output of a mere 10,000 tons in 1925. In contrast, in the 1930's the two quarry companies were dispatching no less than 300,000 tons of stone per annum over the L&CHR. Between the two quarry companies, and about half a mile from the incline, there was a railway company goods shed known simply as "Clee Hill Goods", which received some ordinary incoming freight, including house coal, coke, timber and building materials. The original shed remained in place until at least the 1960's, but the general traffic it was intended to receive seems to have fallen away during the 1950's.

The successful expansion of the quarries on Clee Hill soon encouraged the formation of a company called Field & McKay, to expedite development of a quarry on the nearby Titterstone Clee. In 1880 Field & McKay decided to build another huge incline from Bitterley, but this time on the 3′ gauge. The work was promptly put in hand, and by May, 1881, the Titterstone incline – of comparable length to the Clee Hill incline – was ready for traffic. Unfortunately the first day was marred by an accident which caused considerable damage at the foot of the incline at Bitterley, but mercifully no fatalities. In truth arrangements at Bitterley were not ideal, partly because the site was cramped, and partly because of the difference in gauges. The narrow gauge tracks were installed, parallel to the standard gauge tracks, but at a slightly higher level, thereby enabling Titterstone quarried stone to be unloaded into Field & McKay standard gauge wagons. This location became known as Bitterley wharf, and in or about 1907 a small signalbox was erected, containing 13 levers, the standard gauge layout then being enhanced by the provision of a run-round loop. A few of those employed either at Bitterley or Clee Hill actually lived in Ludlow, and by the 1920's it had been agreed that they could travel to and fro by motorised platelayers' trolley, at no more than 10 mph. This vehicle had to be signalled as if it were a conventional train, and had to carry either the train staff, or ticket, as appropriate.

Above the incline horses appear to have provided all the necessary motive power for some years, but in the Edwardian era Field & McKay expanded their operation by erecting two new stone breaking plants, followed in 1911 by a stone crusher which also screened the broken stone. Increased demand for the product caused the Titterstone East quarry to be opened in October, 1910, situated 1,558 feet above sea level. The steel wagons used on the narrow gauge incline had a capacity of 2 ½ tons, and a "trip" on this incline was limited to a total weight of 15 tons. When fully employed the incline could take up to 40 trips per day, thereby moving up to 600 tons of stone daily. To meet this need Field & McKay acquired a narrow gauge Bagnall saddle tank (1717/1903) in about 1910, and then another from Avonside (1666/1913) about three years later. These engines were employed between the quarries and the incline head, and in 1926 they were supplemented by a tiny vertical boiler shunting locomotive from Sentinel of Shrewsbury (6222/1926). The new arrival was given the name "Lilian", whilst the Avonside was known as "Titterstone", and latterly at least the word was written diagonally across the back of its cab, looking rather more like a brand name than a locomotive name. In 1929 ownership of the quarries and their equipment (including the engines) passed from Field & McKay to the British Quarrying Co. Ltd. The Bagnall saddle tank was scrapped in 1940, but the other two engines survived until the end of the railway on the Titterstone.

At the far end of the line above the Clee Hill incline, lay the screening plant of the Clee Hill Quarry Company, and after World War 1 they acquired for shunting purposes an ungainly but effective Baldwin saddle tank (43201 of 1916), from the Railway Operating Department. For some years this company also had two small 3′ gauge saddle tank engines for work within the quarries, one built by the Falcon Engine Co., and the other by Andrew Barclay. In the meantime the old standard gauge saddle tank No.3243 was retired, and instead the LMS (as successor to the LNWR) decided to experiment with two other small

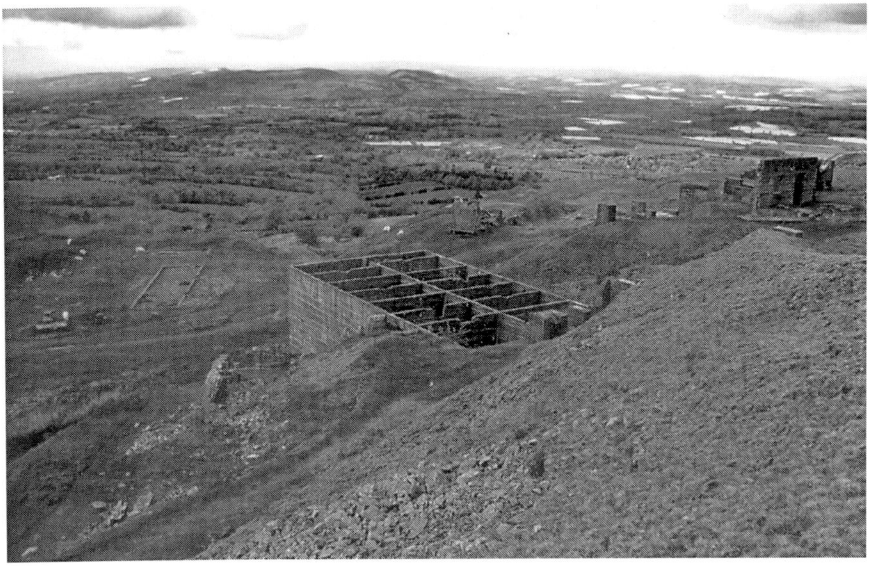

The remains of the stone bins and crushers at the spectacular site on Titterstone Clee in May, 2014. M.R.C. Price

saddle tanks. One was ex-Lancashire & Yorkshire 0-4-0ST 11221, and the other was a former Caledonian 0-4-0ST, 16027 – although some doubt has been expressed as to whether the latter engine ever reached Ludlow, let alone Clee Hill. What is known is that in July, 1931, the LMS ordered a new industrial-type 4 wheel vertical boiler locomotive from Sentinel of Shrewsbury, and that this machine was initially numbered LMS 7164, and later 7184. The Sentinel may have been small, but it was fit for purpose on Clee Hill, and from 1944 to 1946 another Sentinel, LMS 7181 was substituted. After nationalisation in 1948 two more Sentinels, BR numbers 47180 and 47183, had stints on Clee Hill before 7181 – now 47181 – returned. As this locomotive was deemed ripe for retirement in the autumn of 1956, an ex-LNER Sentinel, number 68164, was imported to take care of the traffic. Unfortunately this engine had to be withdrawn after just ten months, and then the decision was taken to bring in ex-GWR 1142, a former Swansea Harbour Trust 0-4-0 ST, built by Hudswell Clarke. The Clee Hill enginemen liked the power this provided, and when it was withdrawn in November, 1959, the replacement was number 1143, another former Swansea Harbour Trust 0-4-0ST, this time built by Peckett. In the event, use of the Peckett was limited, because regular rail traffic above the incline came to an end in May, 1960.

The Clee Hill incline closed officially on 7th September, 1960, but the last wagons were not lowered down the incline until 14th November. On the same day saddle tank 1143 became the last locomotive to make the descent, on its way to the scrapyard. Below the incline the loss of the Titterstone traffic had already reduced the use of Bitterley wharf, and the signalbox had been closed, a small ground frame being installed instead. The surviving quarries on Clee Hill were making increasing use of road transport, and now some stone was brought down to Bitterley wharf by lorry to be put onto the railway.

Between 1960 and 1962 – as for many years previously – trains between Ludlow and Bitterley were worked by robust ex-GWR pannier tanks. This all came to an end with the complete closure of the branch with effect from 15th October, 1962. Track lifting above and below the incline is believed to have taken place by 1964. Today new housing has overwhelmed the site of the junction at Ludlow, and also Middleton siding, whilst the approach to Bitterley has been returned to agriculture, albeit with some engineering brick walls still in evidence. The site of the sidings at Bitterley is now heavily overgrown, but the former wharf is in commercial hands. The incline has returned to the fields from which it was cut, and although the former railway and quarrymens' cottages near the summit are still occupied, the winding house and locomotive shed are long gone. The railway trackbed from the incline top through to the site of Clee Hill goods serves as a public footpath, and although a couple of the older quarries are now flooded, one is still being worked by the Hanson Corporation. Compared to the dust and clatter of past times, Clee Hill is now relatively quiet, although there is ample evidence of former industry. The ruins on Titterstone Clee are particularly striking, as they stand out against a superb view looking towards Ludlow and the Welsh hills beyond.

In conclusion grateful thanks must be expressed to Alf Jenkins and Geoff Cryer for advice in preparation of this appendix, and also to John De Havilland for the accompanying maps.

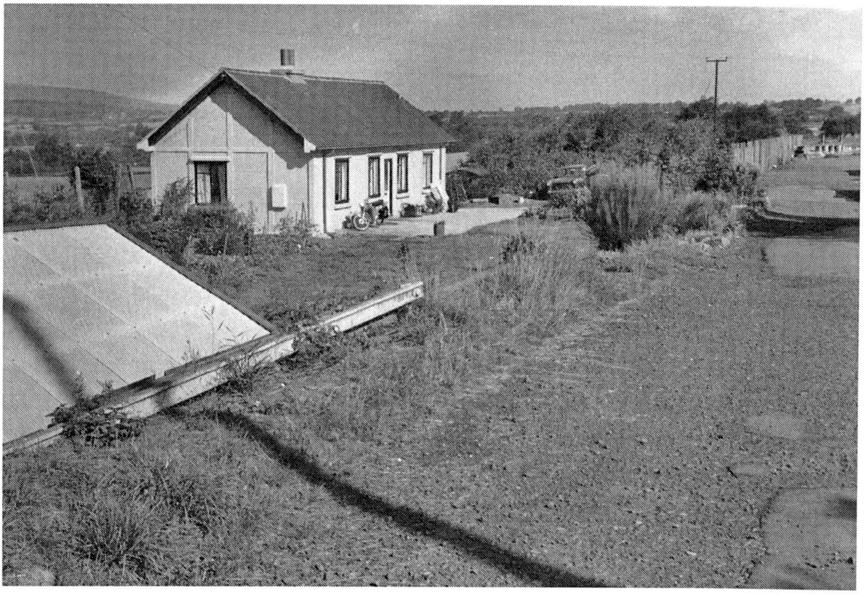

The former station building at Cleobury Town has become a compact bungalow in August, 1975. A length of rail is being used as a boundary marker for the adjacent drive way.

M.R.C. Price

RNAD Ditton Priors Locomotives

The following locomotives are known to have worked at the RNAD, Ditton priors:

		ManufactureDelivered			
	4wDM	FH	2496	1941	New (a)
Yard No. 99	4wDM	RH	221562	1944	From Admiralty, Priddy's Hard (b)
Yard No. DP35	0-4-0DM	RH	313390	1952	New (c)
	0-4-0DM	RH	319286	1953	New (d)
Yard No. DP36	0-4-0DM	RH	375717	1955	New (e)

(a) To RNAD Copperas Wood, Essex.
(b) To RNAD Charlesfield, Roxburghshire *c.*1951.
(c) To RH, late 1965, then to RNAD Broughton Moor, Cumbria, *c.*12/1966.
(d) According to some reports this locomotive arrived at Ditton Priors, but was never off-loaded before moving to another destination. There is now evidence that the locomotive was delivered to Ditton priors in March, 1953, and remained there for sometime – possibly for as long as two years. This locomotive later worked at Priddy's Hard, Gosport.
(e) To RH, late 1965, then to RNAD Eaglescliffe, Co. Durham *c.*6/1966.

At the time of writing two of the locomotives still exist. The Ruston 0-4-0DM No. 313390 is is in preservation with the Kingdom of Fife Railway Preservation Society, still bearing plates identifying it as Yard No. DP35! The very similar locomotive, No. 319286, is preserved on the Northampton and Lamport Railway. It was the first locomotive on the line a donation from Rail & Track supplies Ltd, it is now known as *Sir Gyles Isham* and is still operational.

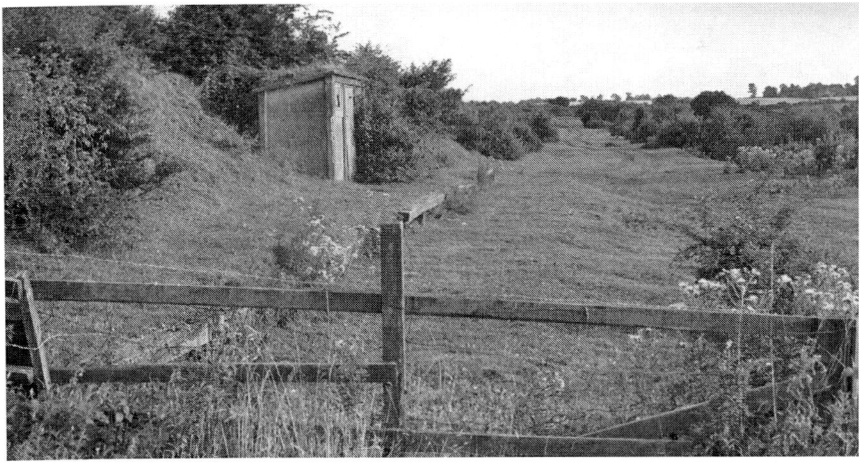

Detton Ford, looking south, 16th August, 1975. *M.R.C. Price*

Bibliography

The Railway Magazine, April 1909
The Locomotive Magazine, 15th June, 1921 (T.R. Perkins)
Locomotion, September 1938
The Railway Magazine, December 1938 (F.G. Richens)
The Great Western Railway Magazine, December 1938
Trains Illustrated, February 1954 (G.F. Bannister)
Steam Days, January-March, 1990 (C. Leigh and A. Muckley)
Back Track, May-June, 1991 (W. Smith)
Cleobury Mortimer & Ditton Priors Light Railway (Oxford Publishing Co., 1980)

Acknowledgements

First and Second Editions

The Naval Armament Supply Officer and Mr J, Harrison-Jones, RNAD, Ditton Priors; BTC Historical Records Department; the *Railway Magazine*; the *Shropshire Magazine*; Lens of Sutton and Weh-Lyn Railway Records; The Birmingham Locomotive Club and Mr E.S. Tonks; Ruston & Hornsby Ltd; the Public Relations Officer, British Railways (W.R.); Viscount Boyne, Mr A.A.G. Delicata, Mrs D. Edwards, Mr A. Hancock, Mr E. Mason, Mr E. Parker and Mr J.V. Vickers.

Third Edition

The Public Record Office, Kew: Shrewsbury Public Library; the GWR Museum, Swindon, and Thamesdown Borough Council; Miss C. Baucutt, Messrs N.L. Allen, R. Daniells, D.G. Geldard, T.J. Edgington, J. de Haviland, N. How, F. Jones, R.W. Kidner, R. Mann, the Mowat Collection and D.J. Powell, R.C. Riley and John Strange.

The Mowat Collection is the property of Brunel University Library but marketed for them by Mr Warwick Burton, 3 Fairway, Clifton, York, YO3 6QA.

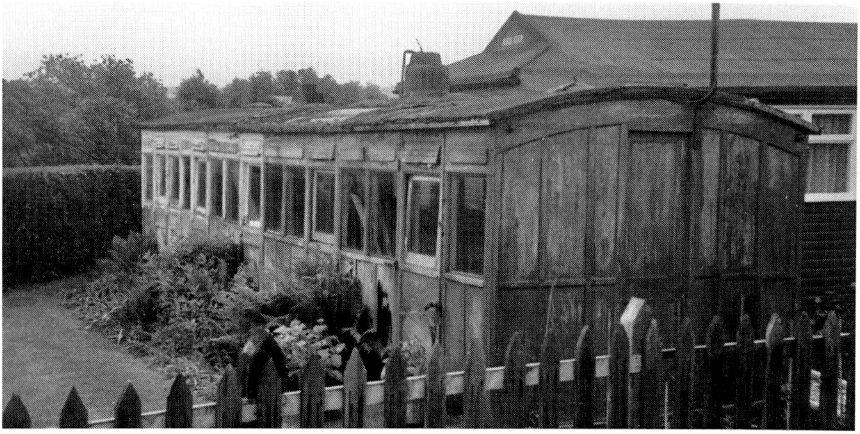

Former CM&DPLR Brake Third coach body at Challow, 1991. This has since been removed. *M.R.C. Price*